How to Record and Mix Great Vocals

MUSICIAN'S GUIDE TO
homerecording

How to Record and Mix
Great Vocals

Craig Anderton

Hal Leonard Books
An Imprint of Hal Leonard LLC

Published in 2018 by Hal Leonard Books
An Imprint of Hal Leonard LLC
7777 West Bluemound Road
Milwaukee, WI 53213

Trade Book Division Editorial Offices
33 Plymouth St., Montclair, NJ 07042

The following photo is provided courtesy of Sweetwater.com: Figures 1.12.

Printed in the United States of America

Book design by NextPoint Training, Inc.

Library of Congress Cataloging-in-Publication Data

Names: Anderton, Craig, author.
Title: How to record and mix great vocals / Craig Anderton.
Description: Montclair, NJ : Hal Leonard Book, 2018. | Series: Musician's guide to home recording | Includes bibliographical references.
Identifiers: LCCN 2018033583 | ISBN 9781540024879
Subjects: LCSH: Popular music--Production and direction. | Sound recordings--Production and direction.
Classification: LCC ML3790 .A644 2018 | DDC 782.049--dc23
LC record available at https://lccn.loc.gov/2018033583

www.halleonardbooks.com

Contents

Acknowledgments

A series like this is never the work of one person, but rather a collection of the experiences obtained over the years from too many people to acknowledge here. Yet some deserve a special mention.

Dan Earley, my editor at Music Sales, who was the first person to say, "You know what would be cool? A series of books on recording, like those Time Life libraries." Well Dan, better late than never, right?

Sir George Martin, who was kind enough to write the foreword to my 1977 book, *Home Recording for Musicians*. He asked for samples of my writing, and I thought that would be the end of it. Instead, he wrote an eloquent foreword that set a wonderful tone for the book. He truly was the consummate gentleman everyone says he was.

The team at Hal Leonard—especially John Cerullo, who green-lighted this series and brought in Frank D. Cook to serve as the editor for these books.

My father, who taught me that it didn't matter if I was a dreadful writer as long as I could edit my words into something readable—and who also showed me what it meant to love music.

My mother, who with my father was unfailingly supportive when I wanted to do things like drop out of college, join a rock band, go on tour, and never look back!

My brother, who understood music on a very deep level and died too young.

And of course, the many *(many)* engineers and producers who let me look over their shoulders and absorb knowledge like a sponge over the past five decades. My hope is that this series will help pass their collective wisdom on to another generation.

Introduction

About This Book

Welcome to the book series Musician's Guide to Home Recording. This series of short publications was written to address the needs of musicians and recording enthusiasts who are interested in creating self-produced songs or doing audio production work for others.

Rather than trying to cover all aspects of recording in a single sprawling volume, each title in the series concisely and accessibly addresses a particular subject. You can select individual titles to hone in on certain skills or proceed through the entire series; this kind of approach lets you develop a comprehensive knowledge at your own pace.

This book, *How to Record and Mix Great Vocals*, covers the art and technology of recording vocals.

The Impact of Great Vocals

The vocal is the most important part of a song: it's the conversation that forms a bond between performer and listener, the element that tells the song's story, and the focus to which other instruments give support.

Technology can't create a great vocal; a performance can. However, what technology can do is take a great performance and make it incredible.

Although this book covers recording, there's more to vocals than tweaking knobs, so it also includes tips on obtaining better performances and discusses how to choose a mic that works well with your voice. And for those who want to dig deeper, I've included "Tech Talk" sidebars with additional information.

Combined with the various techniques and tricks, I hope this book helps you make better, more expressive vocals that leave your listeners amazed and delighted.

How to Use This Book

This book is not about recording vocals with a specific host program, but recording vocals in general. It doesn't go into details on procedures unique to certain programs; however, it does point to where you should look. For example, the book might refer to creating automation to change levels dynamically as needed throughout a song. Although the principles of automation are similar between various programs, the actual procedures may vary somewhat. If you need more details, no worries—just do a search in your program's documentation for automation, and it will describe the procedure you need to use.

Tips and References

This book includes various tips, definitions, cross-references, and other supplemental nuggets throughout its pages. These are denoted with the following icons and formatting.

Tips and side notes provide helpful hints and suggestions, background information, or additional details on a concept or topic.

Definitions provide explanations of technical terms, industry jargon, or abbreviations.

Cross-References alert you to another section, book, or online resource that provides additional information on the current topic.

Chapter 1

Your Mic Is Your Instrument

As a vocalist, your microphone is your instrument. Because it is, you need to love what you use. Some mics will flatter your voice more than others, and some mics can flatter your voice even more with a little equalization (tone control). The mic that sounds best with your voice could be a vintage, really expensive German mic... or a really cheap mic you picked up at a garage sale.

Everyone will give you different advice regarding microphones, so here are my three tips:

- Record yourself singing through a lot of different mics.
- Choose the one you like best (and remember that if one comes close to your ideal sound, signal processing can do a lot to shape the final result).
- The listener won't care what mic you used, as long as they like the vocals.

Getting into all the technical details of microphones is beyond the scope of this book (which is a code phrase authors use—it means "this book is long enough already; I'll never finish it if I add more stuff"). Instead, we'll cover the basics for those who are new to recording vocals; for more information, for more in-depth information, refer to a companion book in the Musician's Guide to Home Recording series, *Microphones for the Recording Musician*.

Really, though, don't believe everything you read or hear about mics. All that matters is that you find a mic that works for you. Best of all, you don't need to know much about the technology behind mics to decide which one(s) sound best with your voice. Use your ears.

Dynamic vs. Condenser Mics

There are two main microphone technologies for vocalists: dyanamic mics and condenser mics. (Ribbon mics are also available, but these are not commonly used for vocals.) Dynamic mics are rugged, require no power, have no internal preamps to generate noise, and are a favorite for live use. They tend to sound not as bright as condenser mics and generally don't provide the same level of detail.

Condenser mics, on the other hand, are the most common mics in the studio and are likely what you'll use. They require power, which is typically +48V. The voltage travels up a mic cable from an audio interface or mixer to the microphone. The nickname for this power source is *phantom power*, because there's no visible power supply—just the cable that makes the audio connection.

If a condenser mic doesn't seem to be working, make sure the phantom power is turned on for the channel the mic is feeding.

Condenser mics can be more sensitive to vocal nuances, have internal electronics, and are somewhat more fragile than dynamic types. However, don't dismiss dynamics mics due to a reputation for being just for live performance—they aren't. A lot of hits were cut with dynamic mics, and one might be the perfect fit for your voice.

Large-Diaphragm vs. Small-Diaphragm Condenser Mics

To generalize, large-diaphragm condenser mics are more sensitive than small-diaphragm condenser mics, but their tone is somewhat less bright. I recommend having both in your collection. I like to record narration through a large diaphragm mic, but do rock vocals with a small diaphragm mic—others might do the reverse, depending on the particular voice. In any case, if you record other acoustic sources, you'll want both types of condenser mics. Choice is good and can add some variety to your signature sound.

The Proximity Effect

I don't want to get geeky, but it's important to recognize that different mics pick up sounds differently due to having different pickup patterns. This can affect how your vocals sound. Omnidirectional-pattern mics pick up any sound hitting them from any direction. Cardioid-pattern mics pick up sounds from the front but not from the back, and bidirectional mics pick up sounds from the front and back, but not the sides. Most vocalists use cardioid mics (see Fig. 1.1).

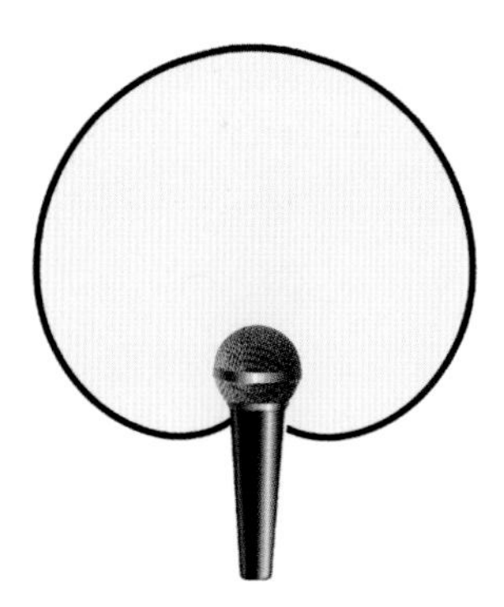

Figure 1.1 A mic's pickup pattern influences how it receives sound. The image is two dimensions, but the pattern is more like a globe surrounding the mic.

Cardioid and other directional pickup patterns exhibit the proximity effect, which means singing closer to the mic doesn't just make the vocal louder, but also more bassy. Vocalists with a thin voice, those who want to present a more intimate vocal, narrators who want to sound like a late-night FM radio DJ, or singers in a Barry White tribute band can use the proximity effect to good advantage.

To reduce the proximity effect, back away a bit from the mic, reduce the bass with equalization (tone control) when mixing your vocal, or use an omnidirectional mic instead. Because an omnidirectional mic picks up sounds from every direction, it doesn't exhibit the proximity effect.

Also note that some mics include a low-frequency roll-off switch. Engaging this switch reduces low frequency response, which can also help reduce the proximity effect (Fig. 1.2).

Figure 1.2 Check if your mic has a low-frequency roll-off switch; this can help minimize unwanted low frequencies.

The Importance of Room Acoustics

You might think that singing close to a mic makes any sound reflections from a room's walls, floor, and ceiling irrelevant, but your room still influences the vocal's sound. Legend has it that the vocal in the classic song "Louie Louie" came from the lead singer shouting upward into a microphone hung from the ceiling.

Although you may be able to use the room sound to good effect, in general you don't want the room sound to have too much of an influence—the more natural the vocal, the more easily you can tweak its sound when mixing. Ways to isolate the mic from room noise include singing in a linen closet (all that soft material dampens the sound), using a screen that blocks reflections from the walls (Fig. 1.3) or spending the bucks for a vocal booth, like the enclosures available from WhisperRoom.

Figure 1.3 The Primacoustic VoxGuard VU minimizes the chance of room reflections getting to the mic.

On the other hand, you may find a room that adds just the right amount of ambience to make your voice sound wonderful. Trust your ears.

Connecting Mics

You will need to connect your mic to an audio interface or other preamp, which requires a suitable cable. As with so many other aspects of audio, people argue for hours about cables. Some people maintain that only the $200/foot cables made out of Venusian unobtainium are acceptable for recording, while others use the cheapest cables they can find.

Cables *can* make a difference, but whether that difference matters often depends on the cable length and its placement in the studio more than anything else. In a typical small studio, where cable runs are short and not draped over items like transformers that generate electric fields, you don't need horribly expensive cables. On the other hand, if you have rare German mics and the world's finest preamps, you may be able to hear a subtle contrast with expensive cables. Realistically, many (if not most) people won't hear a difference.

Professional mics terminate in a male XLR balanced connection; avoid mics with other types of connections. XLR is a type of connector, while balanced wiring is a protocol that minimizes hum and noise pickup when carrying signals.

***XLR* connectors take their name from the Cannon X-series connector with a latching mechanism and a resilient compound around the female contacts.**

The only cable you'll need to record your vocals has a female XLR connector at one end for plugging into a mic and a male XLR connector at the other end for plugging into the audio interface or preamp (Fig. 1.4).

Figure 1.4 A microphone cable has XLR connectors at each end. The top connector is male; the bottom connector is female.

Your audio interface, preamp, or mixer will have XLR microphone inputs (Fig. 1.5).

Figure 1.5 The male XLR connector from the cable (left) plugs into the female mic input (right). This particular audio interface has two microphone inputs.

Tech Talk: Are USB Mics Any Good?

In addition to standard mics with XLR outputs, USB mics are available that plug directly into your computer. These offer some advantages: cables are less expensive, they don't carry audio, and you don't need a traditional audio interface. USB mics got a bad reputation because the earliest models were designed more for convenience or to hit a price point. Most have considerable latency (a delay through your computer system—discussed more in Chapter 2), and the performance was nowhere near a professional level.

However, times have changed, and many USB mics qualify for professional uses such as podcasting. Nonetheless, devices that interface with computers have a disturbing habit of becoming obsolete eventually, whereas XLR mics will continue to be usable for the foreseeable future.

If you need to connect a XLR mic via USB for mobile recording or similar applications, there are XLR to USB converters available, such as Shure's X2u (Fig. 1.6).

Figure 1.6 Several XLR-to-USB converters are available, but avoid the ones with rock-bottom prices—while good for karaoke, don't expect quality from the preamps and converters.

Mic Preamps and Setting Levels

Mics don't generate very strong signals, so they need to be amplified. Any audio interface designed to accommodate mics will include a preamp for each mic input and a gain control to set the amount of amplification. If you're singing directly into a mic, or even if you're several feet away, an audio interface with a mic preamp will have sufficient gain to bring your mic's signal up to acceptable levels for recording.

There are two main types of gain controls, analog and digital. An analog control uses a knob that acts like a standard level control for the analog signal. A digital control uses a knob that doesn't control the audio signal directly, but sets the amount of gain in a preamp. The end result is the same—you can make the mic signal softer or louder—but a digitally controlled mic preamp makes it possible to store repeatable settings, perhaps in an application that comes with your audio interface, or within your recording software (Fig. 1.7).

Figure 1.7 With digital control, in this example, a single knob controls level. The arrow keys choose the preamp whose gain the knob will control, and a separate readout indicates the amount of gain (in this case, 0—the knob hasn't been turned up yet). The lit 48V button indicates that this preamp channel is applying 48V of phantom power to a condenser mic.

Setting Levels

Virtually all audio interfaces and preamps provide input level metering, but the sophistication varies. There's even some question as to how necessary input meters are—after all, you may not be able to adjust the input level in the recording software itself, so you'll adjust the audio interface's input levels based on the recording software's meters or a mixer application that comes with the audio interface.

The simplest indicator is a single LED or other indicator to show *clipping*. If a meter shows a red clipping indicator, then you would simply turn down the mic gain control on your audio interface until the clip LED doesn't light on peaks.

Clipping: **A condition caused when an input signal has exceeded the available headroom and will therefore be distorted.**

The next step up is more than one LED, or a bi-color LED to indicate green for signal present and red for clipping. The signal present LED is helpful if you're not seeing audio going to your recording program. That way you can determine whether the problem is the signal going to the interface—maybe you forgot to turn on phantom power for a condenser mic. Or perhaps you have an incorrect setting inside the software itself—like forgetting to arm the track for recording.

Multi-stage meters are also available with three or more indicators to show a series of levels (Fig. 1.8).

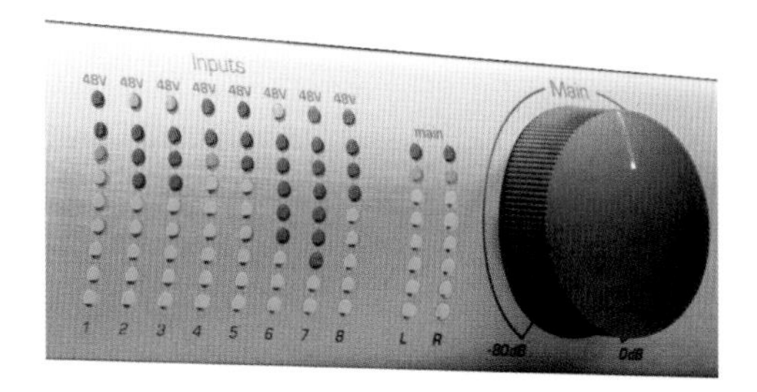

Figure 1.8 The PreSonus Studio 192 has eight-step meters for all eight analog input channels, as well as indicators to show which channels are receiving 48V phantom power. Note the topmost LED in the meter for Input 1 is red, which means the input is clipping and its gain needs to be turned down.

Make sure you don't turn up the gain too high—leave enough headroom when you set levels to accommodate sudden volume peaks. Remember, you can always raise the gain of sections with low levels, but if you sing the vocal of your life and it's distorted because the gain was too high, there's little you can do about it after the fact.

Mic Preamp Low Cut and Phase Switches

Low-cut switches can reduce pops and other low-frequency artifacts you'll want to get rid of while recording. As mentioned previously, some mics include a roll-off switch. Functionally similar switches are sometimes included in an audio interface's preamps (as with the Focusrite Clarett 8PreX; see Fig. 1.9). These can minimize pops and booms prior to the A/D converters. This allows for more headroom and may help prevent distortion.

Figure 1.9 The Focusrite Clarett 8PreX has front-panel hardware switches for low cut (to the right of the 48V phantom power switch) and phase (to the right of the low-cut switch).

Phase switches flip the phase (also called polarity) of the mic signal. Although theoretically this shouldn't make a difference with mono signals like voice, you can run into an issue when using two (or more) mics on the same signal source, like a group of background singers. If mixing the signals from the two mics together in mono produces a weaker or thinner sound, reverse the phase of one of the mics and decide if that improves the sound. Note that you can typically reverse phase in your host software as well, but recording with the proper phase relationship means one less item to consider when mixing.

Remote Control

If you're engineering yourself, you're probably sitting fairly close to your computer and dealing with fan and other computer-related noises, or you've set up your mic far enough away to avoid noise—but you then have to run back and forth between the mic and the interface to tweak levels, as well as the program to make any needed settings.

Fortunately, several programs offer remote control applications for iOS and/or Android devices (Fig. 1.10).

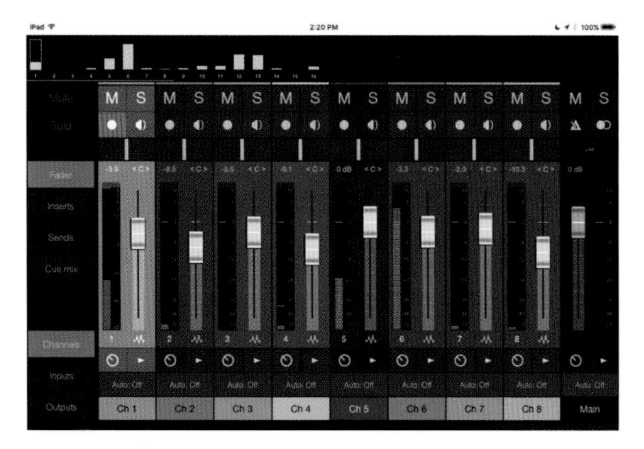

Figure 1.10 This remote application for PreSonus Studio One allows running the transport and setting levels remotely, which simplifies recording away from noise sources.

If your software doesn't have a remote control application, another option is to use a wireless QWERTY computer keyboard and to learn the keyboard shortcuts necessary for recording vocals (record, stop, etc.). You can typically be at least 20 feet away, even if there's a wall between you and the wireless keyboard receiver.

***Wireless keyboard receiver*: A (typically) small device that plugs into a computer's USB port to receive the signal transmitted by the keyboard.**

Are Mic Preamps Really that Different?

This is yet another topic where audio enthusiasts can argue about minute sonic differences. Are $4,000 preamps nice? Yes, they are. Alfa Romeos are nice too, but even the least expensive Ford Focus will get you where you want to go. There are quite a few good low-cost preamps, and a great vocal performance will make it intact through any of them. When *Sound on Sound* magazine conducted a mic preamp shootout where participants didn't know what they were listening to, the unit judged as sounding the best by most listeners was a relatively inexpensive mic preamp you could pick up at any music store.

To be fair, there used to be bigger differences between expensive and inexpensive gear. These days, though, the audio quality in general has improved dramatically. Even the mic preamps found in inexpensive computer interfaces can have very respectable specifications. If you own a decent audio interface, don't obsess about the preamps—they're fine. Sure, throw more money at your gear if you want, but first do a blind test to compare what you have with what you're buying. You might be surprised at the results.

Accessories

Mics do not exist in isolation, so here are some of the most common accessories.

Pop Filters

When you sing close to any kind of mic, the bursts of air from plosives (*b*, *p*, and similar sounds) can overload the mic and produce unpleasant, low-frequency popping sounds. A pop filter places a fine mesh (metal or plastic) between the vocalist and mic to help diffuse these bursts of air. Although some engineers feel pop filters detract from a vocal, pops can detract from a vocal even more. If you don't need a pop filter, that's probably because you're singing quite a distance from the mic, or are very careful about where you aim your voice when you're singing. (Aiming somewhat below the mic helps reduce pops.) When mixing, you can use equalization to reduce pops, but a pop filter minimizes the problem at the source. Engaging a mic's low-frequency roll-off switch can also help reduce pops.

Pop filters range from really cheap (an old nylon stocking stretched on a hanger in front of the mic) to really expensive. Most pop filters run between $20 and $100, and they'll do the job to one degree or another. However, one day I tried a $300 PaulyTon Pauly SuperScreen pop filter and realized why it cost so much (see Fig. 1.11). Compared to regular pop filters, it was like the difference between flying first class on Virgin Air compared to flying Southwest.

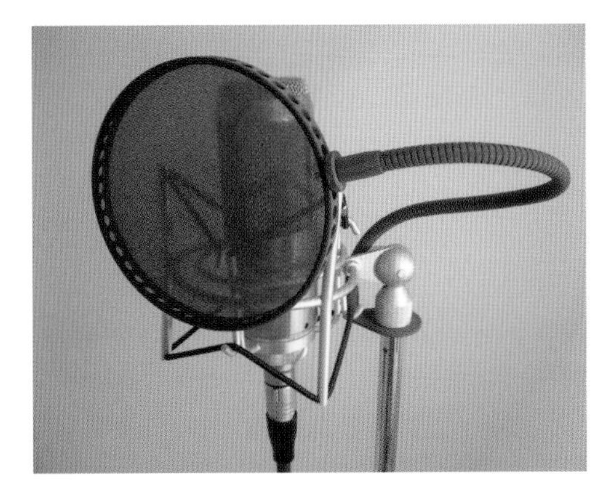

Figure 1.11 The PaulyTon Pauly SuperScreen is super expensive—but also super effective.

Mic Stand

Unless you intend to hold your mic at all times, you'll need a mic stand. These sell at all price points, from $20 to hundreds of dollars, but it's often worth spending a bit more for something really solid. Putting a heavy mic on a budget mic stand can cause it to be unstable—and you don't want your precious mic crashing to the floor when a stand tips over! Having a boom extension is handy for uses other than vocals, such as miking an acoustic guitar for a performer who is sitting down (Fig. 1.12).

Figure 1.12 This K&M mic stand has a boom attached at the top to make it easy to position the mic when miking various instruments.

Also note that if you plan to sing while at your mixer or by your computer, you can get a desk stand designed for applications like broadcasting that are inexpensive and don't take up much space.

Shock Mount

A shock mount isolates the mic from a mic stand, which can be very important if other sound sources are present in the room. Because a mic stand sits on the floor, any vibrations from the floor (like those caused by moving your feet or sounds from other instruments) can transfer up the stand to the mic and add low-frequency artifacts. A low-cut switch can help with this, but it's better to isolate the mic as much as possible using shock mounts. These are often included with a mic as part of the package (Fig. 1.13).

Figure 1.13 The shock mount on the left is included with the Neat Microphones Worker Bee, which is inserted in the mount. The shock mount on the right is for an Audio-Technica AT3035.

Protective Box or Pouch

Good microphones are a significant investment, so you want to take care of them. Mics don't like dust or being dropped, so it's helpful to put them away when not in use. Most mics come with some kind of pouch or case for storage or transport (Fig. 1.14).

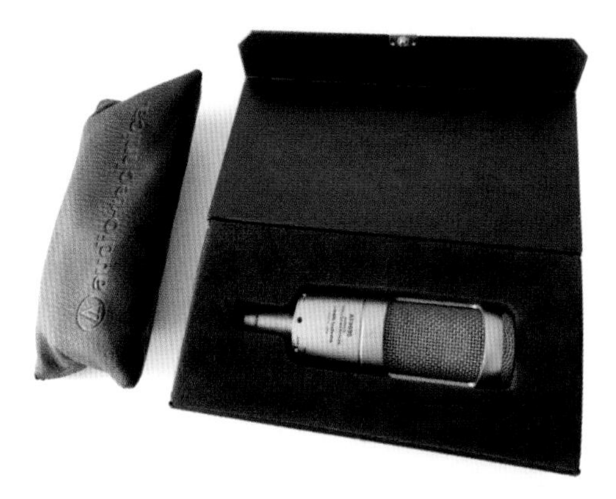

Figure 1.14 The pouch on the left comes with Audio-Technica's AT2020USB mic, which is a USB mic designed for musicians on the go. The box on the right protects Audio-Technica's AT3035 condenser mic in the studio.

If you have mics set up in the studio and don't want to put them away because they're placed right where you want them, simply take a non-porous plastic bag, turn it upside down, and cover the mic temporarily to keep dust out of it.

Headphones

It may seem odd to include headphones as an accessory, but you'll need to monitor tracks as you sing. Look for headphones that are comfortable and lightweight, and that cover your ears to avoid sound leakage into your mic. My go-to phones are KRK's KNS 8400 (Fig. 1.15), not only because they meet all those requirements and sound great, but because they include a volume slider in the cable that makes it very easy to adjust the monitoring level while singing.

Figure 1.15 Choose your headphones carefully, because you don't want them to be an annoyance while you sing. The KNS 8400 headphones were designed specifically for studio rather than consumer applications.

Key Takeaways

- Try out a bunch of mics to find out which sounds best with your voice. You'll likely end up with a condenser mic.
- Try to sing in a space that's not influenced by the room sound.
- Be careful not to set the gain too high—if the vocal distorts, there's not much you can do to fix it afterward.
- Look for remote control for your recording software and/or interface; this can be extremely handy if you're engineering yourself.
- Don't obsess over mic preamps—almost all of them are at least good enough. The vocalist will be the limiting factor on most vocals, not the preamp.
- Accessorize with a pop filter if you encounter problems with plosives. Also use quality cables and mic stands.
- Don't pay too much attention to what you read on the net about mics—I guarantee none of the writers are using your particular voice! If a mic doesn't flatter your voice, find one that does.

Chapter 2

Recording Techniques

Hard disk recording techniques have affected every aspect of recording, including vocals. Although overdubbing vocals (recording another vocal over an existing vocal) and punch recording (re-recording and replacing a section of a vocal) have been common techniques for years, today's software programs let you create multiple tracks of vocals and make a single composite track with all the best bits. For example, you can keep the beginning from one take, the middle from a different take, and the end from yet another take. Let's look at all the ways you can record with today's hard disk recording programs.

To Hold or Not to Hold?

Most recording engineers use a mic stand to prevent the vocalist from creating extraneous handling noise when holding the mic. But personally, I just can't sing that way—I have to hold the mic to get a good performance, because I like to move around. Besides, I need to move the mic farther away when I sing louder, and closer when I need more intimacy. And the handling noise isn't really that bad if you're careful.

So I say, if you want to hold the mic, go ahead and hold it! Just remember, you may end up recording some noise that you don't want.

DPA Microphones makes the d:facto 4018 Vocal Mic, which is designed to minimize handling noise. It's an excellent microphone, although it is pricey.

Mic Technique

It's good to get carried away with your performance, but do try to reserve some concentration for making your audio happy. The most natural, artifact-free, and super-low-cost dynamics-control processor is great mic technique—moving closer for more intimate sections and farther away when singing more forcefully. This can go a long way toward reducing the need for drastic electronic compression.

Compression is discussed in detail in Chapter 5 of this book.

Monitoring Your Vocals

While you sing, you'll want to hear what you're singing. The usual procedure is to listen to a mix of the existing tracks through headphones, and sing along with that. But everyone has a different approach to what works best for them.

I use closed earphones (open-air types are an invitation to leakage), with one cup firmly on one ear, and the other halfway on. I then put little, if any vocal into the headphone monitor mix (except when adding an overdub to an existing part, in which case I monitor the previous vocal a little higher than usual).

Some audio interfaces include signal processing that lets you monitor your voice through EQ, compression, reverb, etc., but you don't have to record these effects. Personally, I find this gives me a false sense of security. For example, if compression evens out my voice, it's harder to tell if I'm singing with a consistent level. If I listen to my voice without processing, it forces me to work at better and more consistent singing. However, if you prefer to hear some reverb in the headphones to feel more comfortable—and you therefore create a better vocal—then crank up that reverb.

Recording a Vocal

This is where it all starts, and here's how you do it (Fig. 2.1).

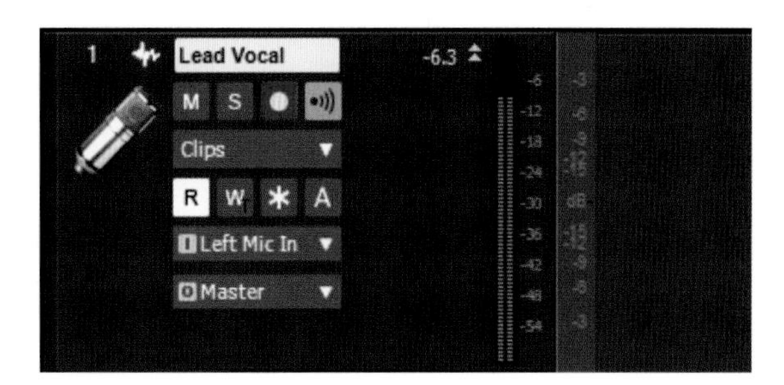

Figure 2.1 A vocal track ready to record

1. Create an audio track. Typically this will be a mono track, but some programs don't differentiate between mono and stereo tracks.

2. Set the track input to use the audio interface input that's carrying your mic's audio. In the screenshot, the input (I) has been set to the left channel of an audio interface's stereo input, which, because it's mono, feeds the track's left and right channels (this is why you see signal in both meter channels).

3. Set the audio interface or preamp levels to avoid distortion. As mentioned previously, you want the maximum level short of distortion—but make sure you leave some extra headroom, just in case. Here, the meter shows that the signal peaks are hitting –6.3 dB.

4. Enable the *arm recording* button, which lights red (this is also called record-enabling a track).

5. If you want to monitor the input signal through your software, enable the *input monitor* function. In this case, it's the orange button. Some programs refer to this function as *echo input.* If your audio interface offers zero-latency monitoring, you can monitor the signal going into the interface instead of hearing it through the computer, which adds *latency* (delay). Consult your audio interface documentation for how to do this.

6. Click Record in your transport... and away you go!

Tech Talk: Zero-Latency Monitoring

Latency refers to the delay that affects an audio signal when passing through a computer system. In a system with latency, if you're monitoring your computer's output, there will be a delay between the time you sing a note and the time you hear it in the monitors or headphones. This delay can be disconcerting.

Modern audio interfaces and computers have made latency almost a thing of the past, but because it still can be an issue, some audio interfaces include a feature called *zero-latency monitoring* or *direct monitoring.* This reduces latency to virtually nothing, so what you hear as you monitor is essentially in real time. However, it does this by monitoring the signal at your audio interface's audio input, thus bypassing the computer completely—it's as if you used a Y-cable and sent one feed to the audio interface and the other one to your monitor speakers or headphones.

If you are running your vocal through a plug-in running inside the computer, like reverb, delay, or compression, you won't hear it if you select zero-latency monitoring. On the other hand, if you want to hear yourself in the headphone with no latency, zero-latency monitoring is very useful. Also, some audio interfaces include effects that you can listen to while singing that won't be recorded on the track.

Overdubbing Vocals

Overdubbing means singing along with an existing vocal on a separate track. For example, you might want to overdub a harmony. The procedure for overdubbing is the same as for recording, because you're recording to a new track. You'll want to monitor the previous track so you can sing along with it.

Punching Vocals

Punching refers to overwriting a section of an existing vocal with a new section. This is a great solution if you sing a vocal perfectly except for one small phrase; you can record over just that one phrase until it's right, without having to re-record the entire vocal.

Back in the days of tape recording, punching was a demanding art. While the tape was rolling, the engineer would have to punch in and out at the exact right time—usually in the spaces between words or phrases.

Situations that required punching an individual word or partial phrase were very difficult. Any mistake that cut off part of the vocal you didn't want to lose meant you were out of luck—there was no undo button.

With today's software, you can set up punch-in and punch-out points exactly where you want them. You start the transport from before the punch-in point. When the transport reaches the punch-in point, the track starts recording for the new vocal. When the transport reaches the punch-out point, recording stops. (Fig. 2.2). If you don't like the results, you can simply hit undo and try again.

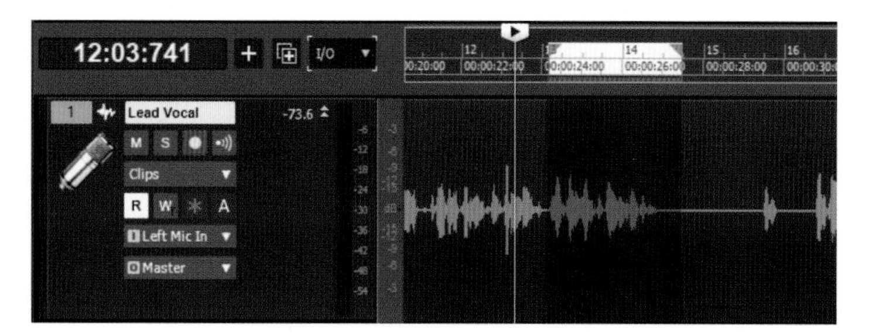

Figure 2.2 The red indicators in the timeline show the punch-in and punch-out points. When the line that shows the current location in the song goes past the punch-in point, recording will begin.

As with so many functions, different programs handle punching differently (for example, some erase the previous track immediately, some only after the transport passes the punch-in point). Although composite recording (see next) is the way many people record vocals these days, for a quick touch-up to a part, punching is often the fastest solution.

Composite Vocals

Composite vocals piece together the best parts of multiple takes into a single performance. Some producers feel that creating composite vocals doesn't produce as natural a feel as a take that goes all the way through from beginning to end, while others believe that being able to choose from multiple takes can give a vocal more range and interest than might occur within a single take. My preference is to keep the composite sections as long as possible rather than slice and dice every word, but certain hit singers *do* slice and dice almost every word... and with platinum records on the wall, I'm not about to say they're wrong.

When creating composite vocals, if at all possible, record all the takes at the same time, using the same mic, mic position, mixer settings, etc. If you record additional parts later, it will be hard to match the timbres and levels of previously recorded parts.

Following are the basic steps involved in creating composite vocal tracks, often called *comping* for short.

Record the Takes

When comping, be sure to record enough takes so there's plenty of material to piece together a good performance. (*Loop recording* is particularly handy when doing vocal comps.) While you're in a recording mood, record at least several seconds of a track without singing into the mic—be as quiet as possible. This audio can be handy to have around, for reasons described later.

Tech Talk: Loop Recording Vocals

This process repeats a section of music over and over while the vocalist sings a new vocal during each pass. Each vocal pass goes on its own track, playlist, or take. Previous takes are muted while the singer records the current pass. Loop recording vocals allows the vocalist to get comfortable with the part and try different approaches. The end result is multiple versions of the vocal, from which it's easy to audition and select the best sections.

Audition the Takes

Once you have several tracks of vocals, you can split each track into phrases (or pieces of phrases, if appropriate). Next, solo a track with a phrase, and listen to the phrase; then solo other tracks with the same phrase. Determine which is the best one. Some software lets you mute individual phrases, which means you can mute everything except for the best parts as you play through the vocal.

I recommend setting *loop start* and *loop end* points around phrases so you can listen to them repeatedly. (Loop points set a start point and end point for playback; when the track reaches the end point, playback resumes from the start point ad infinitum until stopped.) Some programs let you *scrub* (drag across and hear sound) for particular sections, and there are other ways to audition clips as well. Choose the method that fits your working style best.

Now repeat this auditioning procedure, phrase by phrase, until you've reviewed the entire performance and found the best sections (Fig. 2.3).

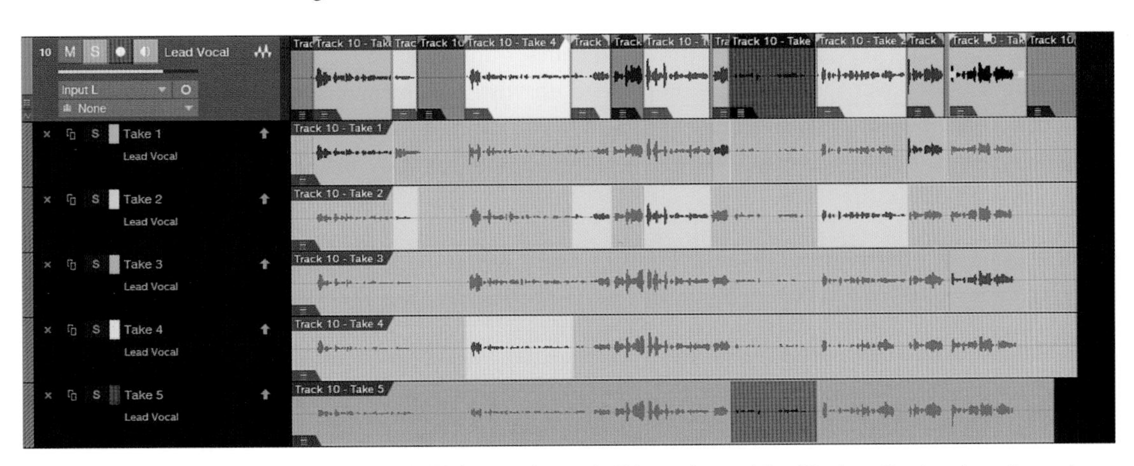

Figure 2.3 The highlighted phrases in Takes 1 through 5 have been identified as the best parts and promoted to the main track where they can then be bounced (combined) into the final composite part.

Note that most recording software has a function called *dim solo.* This lets you solo a track and still hear the non-soloed tracks played back at a lower level. This type of solo is helpful when compositing vocals, because you can hear the phrase under review in context with the rest of the song. Listening to vocals out of context—i.e., listening to the vocal line in isolation—can produce nasty surprises when you put the vocals back in context with the rest of the tracks.

Check the Flow

Composite vocals can indeed produce "perfect" vocals. But perfection isn't always more important than flow. A line in the movie *Spice World* sums it up, where someone working with the Spice Girls says, "That was absolutely perfect... without being actually any good."

The Spice Girls are an all-female pop group from the mid-90s.

Very few vocalists are accomplished enough to maintain the same flow through multiple takes of a tune. In the same vein, there's a moment at 4:38 in Madonna's song "Ray of Light" where she doesn't quite hit the note sequence. She could have fixed it, or punched over it, but she didn't. As a result, it comes across with a sense of approaching something edgy (maybe ecstatic, maybe dangerous) *far* better than if she had hit each pitch perfectly.

Listen carefully to your vocal from start to finish to make sure it flows well from an *artistic* standpoint. One mistake some people make is to choose the best phrases from only a *technical* standpoint; this can lead to an overly uniform (translation: *boring*) vocal. For example, sometimes you might deliberately choose a less expressive rendition of a line if it comes just before an emotional high point, thus heightening the contrast.

Another option to create a well-flowing part takes more work, but can be very effective. After assembling your perfect track, listen to it repeatedly—say, 10 or 20 times—until you've learned the composite version. Then try recording the part over again. At best, you'll end up with a performance that flows better than the composite because you'll be totally comfortable with it. Or you might end up with a part that's suitable for doubling. While it might not be as perfect as the composite, doubling may help obscure some of the cut-and-paste nature of the composite track.

Now that you've decided what to keep, delete everything that's not going to be part of the final vocal. Some people keep everything with hard disk recording, just because they can. But there's no need to keep sections you've rejected (Fig. 2.4). You rejected them for a reason, right?

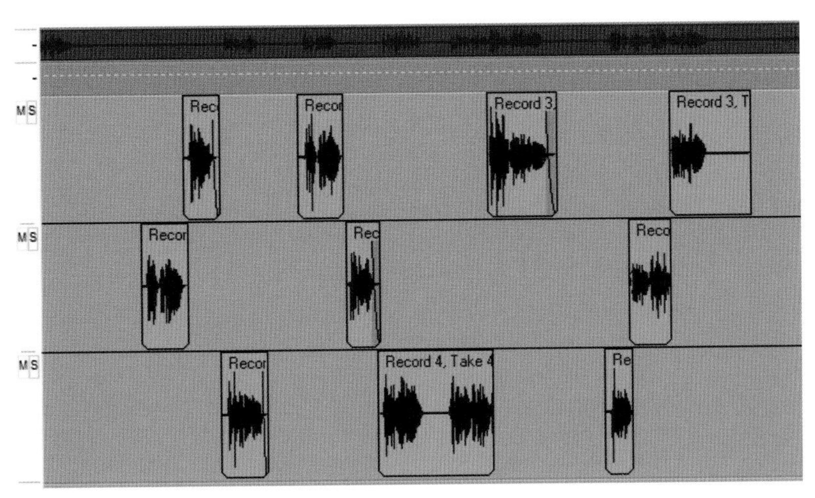

Figure 2.4 This composite vocal has weeded out the unwanted clips so only the best parts remain from three different takes. They can then be bounced together into a single part.

Bounce the Takes Together

This isn't absolutely necessary, but combining all the bits into a single track (a process called *bouncing*) can simplify subsequent editing and processing. However before bouncing, you should play the song through from start to finish and match the levels of the vocal segments as closely as possible.

After everything's set, implement the program's bounce or mix-to-hard-disk function. You can typically bounce to an empty track, bounce the segments together in an existing track, or export the audio to disk and import it back into the project. After the vocals are done, check how your program deals with deleting unused pieces of audio, because deleting rejected parts of takes can reclaim significant space from your hard drive.

The Next Step

Now you're ready to edit the vocal—however you obtained it—with your recording software's DSP functions and effects. But please remember that it's very difficult to edit your way to a good performance. While you can often edit a good performance into an excellent performance, editing can reach a point of diminishing returns pretty quickly.

DSP **stands for digital signal processing. Here we use the term to mean general computer-based signal manipulation for processing audio and applying effects.**

Make sure you have the performance you want before proceeding, and remember the suggestion about re-recording the performance after you've bounced—you might end up with something a whole lot better than you're liable to get from a Frankenpart.

Key Takeaways

- There's no law against holding a mic when you're singing if that makes you more comfortable, but be careful to avoid handling noise.
- Learn good mic technique and you won't have to fix levels after the fact.
- Find the way to monitor your vocals that works best for you—whether listening to your voice in the headphones, having no voice in the headphones, or finding a balance somewhere in between.
- Sometimes punch recording over a section that needs to be re-done is quicker than doing composite recording.
- When choosing elements of a composite vocal, consider the overall flow—not just whether individual sections are technically perfect.
- Listen to the various takes in context with the music, not as isolated vocal lines.
- Loop recording is a great way to capture your vocals. It also gives you the freedom to try out different parts and later evaluate them in context with the song.

Chapter 3

Preparing Your Vocals for the Mix

By now you've found the perfect mic for your voice, caught the emotion, remembered to use a pop filter, and even did a little composite recording to get the best takes. So you have a great performance in your recording software and it's time to mix, right?

Actually, no—it's time to prep your vocals to get them ready for the mix. The type of editing we're about to explore involves a fair amount of detail work, and it can easily take an hour to optimize a complete vocal. So is it necessary, you ask? I think the results are worth it. A smooth, consistent, performance that hasn't had the life compressed out of it gives the vocal more importance—and as far as I'm concerned, there's no more important element of any song than the lead vocal.

Step 1: Remove Hiss

This is an advanced technique, and fortunately, not always necessary—but if you need to remove hiss, you should take care of it before doing anything else. Ideally, you won't have much noise, but vocal tracks often exhibit some degree of preamp hiss, hum, and the like. Removing the hiss can make for a more open vocal sound: it's like removing a layer of dust from a painting.

Once the performance is done, I like to bounce the vocal into one long track that lasts from the start of the song to the end. Next, I export it for importing into a digital audio editing program that has the ability to do noise reduction. For example, Magix Sound Forge, Adobe Audition, and Steinberg WaveLab each have built-in noise reduction algorithms. Stand-alone audio restoration programs are also available, including iZotope RX (see Fig. 3.1) and the free ReaFIR plug-in for Windows from Cockos.

The documentation for each of these programs will go into detail on how to use them to reduce noise, but the general procedure is the same. First, find a section of the recording that consists of only noise; next, save that as a reference sample called a *noiseprint*; then instruct the program to subtract anything with those characteristics from the vocal.

Remember the advice in Chapter 2 to record a little bit of residual noise, with no vocal? It could come in handy now to provide a suitable noiseprint.

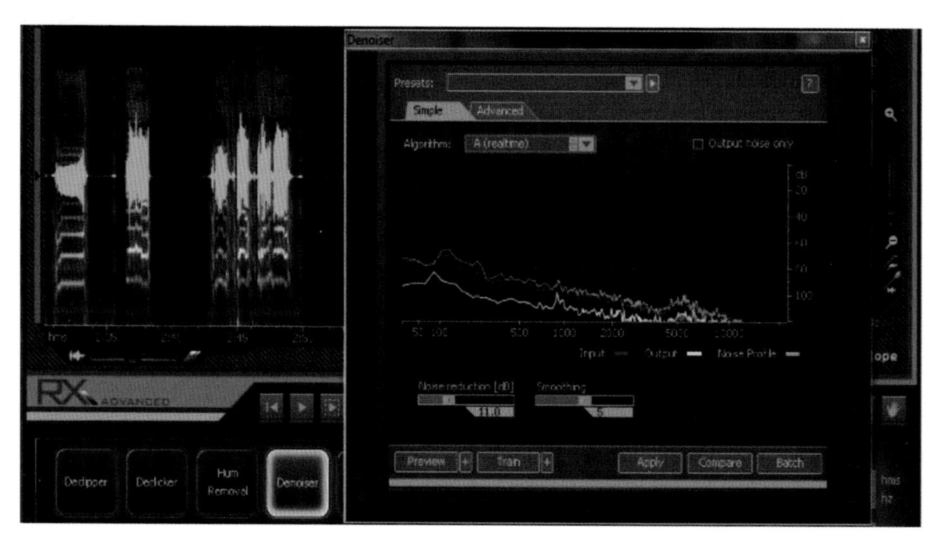

Figure 3.1 The lower section of the Denoiser window in iZotope RX shows the noiseprint of the hiss that's about to be removed.

Two cautions apply with this procedure: First, sample only the noise (a few hundred milliseconds will be enough), and second, don't apply too much noise reduction—6 to 10 dB should be sufficient. If you are too aggressive, you may either remove parts of the vocal itself or introduce artifacts, both of which will create an artificial sound.

Step 2: Delete Silences

After reducing the overall hiss level, delete all the sections between vocal passages. By doing this, the voice will mask any noise where it's present, and where there's no voice, you'll have no noise at all from headphone leakage, mouth noises, mic handling, etc.

One option for removing sound in the vocal-free areas is to use a noise gate plug-in to remove audio below a specified level. This process silences the track's audio when its level drops below a set threshold, and passes it through when the level is above the threshold. Thus, you won't hear low-level hiss and noise, but you will hear the vocal itself.

For a detailed discussion on noise gates, please see Chapter 5 in this book.

While this semi-automated process saves time, the most flexible—although the most tedious—option is to make these changes manually by editing. This involves cutting the spaces between vocals, then adding fade-ins and fade-outs to smooth the transitions between the vocal and silence (see Fig. 3.2).

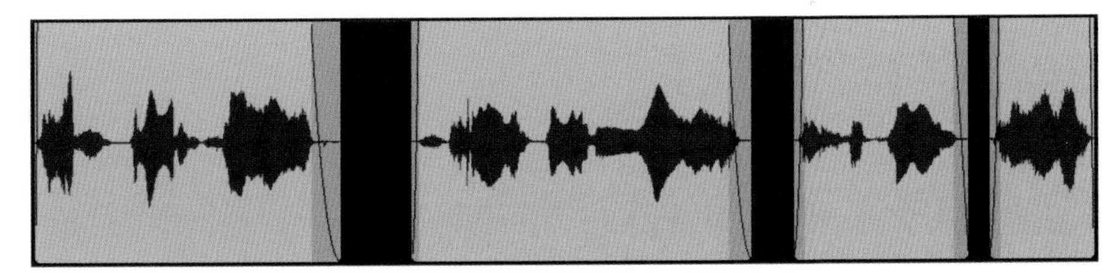

Figure 3.2 The spaces between vocal phrases have been removed and fades added to create smooth transitions.

Also consider inserting a steep high-pass filter (48 dB per octave, if available) to cut the low frequencies below the voice (e.g., below 80 Hz or so). This is where subsonics, hum, mud, and plosive pops live.

For more detail on equalization, see Chapter 4 of this book.

And while you're applying fades, focus some attention on sustained notes with doubled vocals. You can line up the fade-outs on the two vocal tracks to ensure that they end together. This gives a more cohesive, tight vocal sound.

Step 3: Reduce Breath Noises and Inhales

Breath inhales are a natural part of the vocal process, so you don't want to remove them entirely. For example, an obvious inhale cues the listener that the subsequent vocal section is going to be a little more intense.

That said, applying any compression later on will amplify low level signals. This will bring up the levels of any vocal artifacts—possibly to the point of being objectionable. To reduce the level of inhales, define the region with the inhale and reduce the gain by 3 to 7 dB or so. This is usually done using DSP or a clip envelope. A small amount of reduction will allow you to retain the inhale's essential character, but make it less obvious compared to the vocal (see Fig. 3.3).

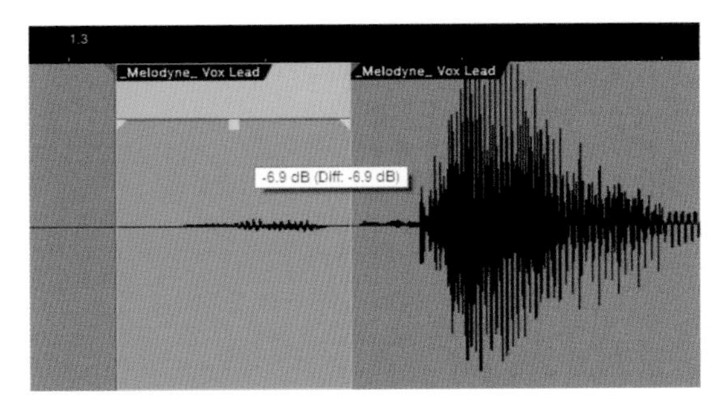

Figure 3.3 The highlighted clip contains a prominent inhale, so the clip gain has been reduced by 6.9 dB to make the inhale less conspicuous—but not eliminate it completely.

Tech Talk: Clip Envelopes

A clip envelope allows making changes to level, pan, and sometimes other characteristics within an audio clip. The envelope starts off as a straight line. In the case of level, you can raise or lower the line to raise or lower the level, respectively. You can also make changes to just a section of the line, like lowering the section that extends for the duration of the breath inhale while leaving the rest of the level untouched.

Step 4: Reduce Plosive Severity

When a pop filter doesn't take out all of a plosive, a brute force method can reduce it further. This involves applying a steep high-pass filter that removes low frequencies where plosives occur. You can often (but not always) apply this to an entire vocal track, because filtering out the frequencies below the vocal range may be sufficient. Note that you can insert multiple high-pass filters in series to make the cutoff below the vocal range steeper—kind of like a virtual pop filter.

If you need to apply the filter more selectively, you have two common options. One is to split the vocal clip to separate the part with the plosive and insert a high-pass filter only in that clip. However, not all software allows for inserting an effect like a filter into an audio clip, so in this case you will need to move the split clip (and any other clips that contain plosives) to a separate track, and add the filter effect to the entire track.

Reducing the lows sufficiently to remove the pop may also thin the voice somewhat as well. A better, albeit more time-consuming option is to zoom in on the plosive (it will have a distinctive waveform that you'll learn to recognize); then split the clip just *before* the pop. Next, add a fade-in over the pop. The fade-in's duration will determine the pop's severity—the longer the fade, the less pop. So you can fine-tune the desired amount of "p" sound you want to let through by adjusting the fade length (see Fig. 3.4).

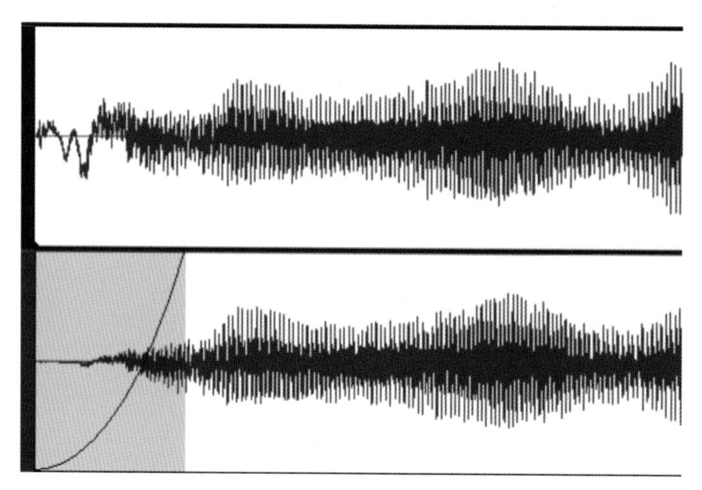

Figure 3.4 The clip on the top shows a nasty pop. The lower clip fades in over the pop to reduce its intensity.

Step 4: Phrase-by-Phrase Normalization/Gain Changes

Unless you have the mic technique of a k. d. lang, the odds are that some phrases will be softer than others—not intentionally due to natural dynamics, but as a result of poor mic technique, running out of breath, or not being able to hit one note as strongly as other notes. Compression used to even out a vocal's peaks certainly has its place—but the low-level sections might not be affected very much, whereas the high-level areas will sound "squashed."

To retain more overall dynamics, it can be better to edit the vocal to a consistent level first, before applying any compression. One way to do this is with phrase-by-phrase *normalization* or gain changes. Normalization raises selected audio so that its peak level reaches a specified level. Typically this is the maximum available headroom (especially with narration), but that's not always the best option. For example, if a vocal is too soft but part of that is due to natural dynamics, you can normalize to, say, –3 dB or so in comparison to the rest of the vocal's peaks (see Fig. 3.5).

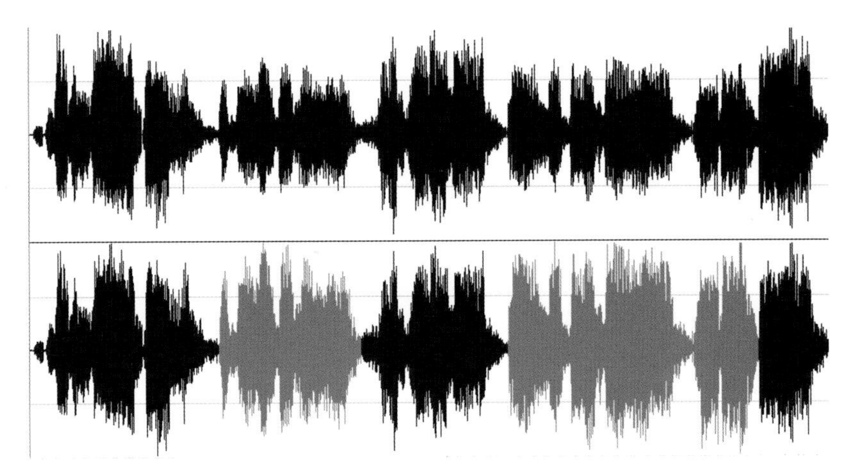

Figure 3.5 The upper waveform is the original waveform; the lower one uses gain changes (highlighted in purple) to raise the level of lower-level phrases.

If you need to add an element of expressiveness later on that wasn't in the original vocal (for example, if the song gets softer in a particular place, so you need to make the vocal softer), you can do this with judicious use of automation.

Automation is discussed in Chapter 7 of this book.

The advantage of adjusting each phrase's level for consistency is that you won't add any of the artifacts associated with compression, nor interfere with a phrase's inherent dynamics. So even though the vocal will be more present and consistent, it will sound completely natural. Furthermore if you *do* add compression or limiting while mixing, you won't need to use as much as you otherwise would to obtain the same degree of perceived volume. Just be careful not to get so involved in this process that you start normalizing granular elements, like individual words. Within any given phrase there will be some dynamics that you'll want to retain.

A side benefit of phrase-by-phase normalization is you can define a region that starts just after an inhale, to avoid bringing up the inhale with the rest of the phrase. One potential problem can occur if the region you're processing isn't bounded by silence, but instead has audio continuing either before or after the boundaries. An abrupt level change can cause a click where the transition occurs. Some recording programs introduce automatic, short crossfades when processing a section of the audio, which usually solves this problem. You can also add your own crossfades or extend an automatic crossfade to make for a smoother transition (see Fig. 3.6).

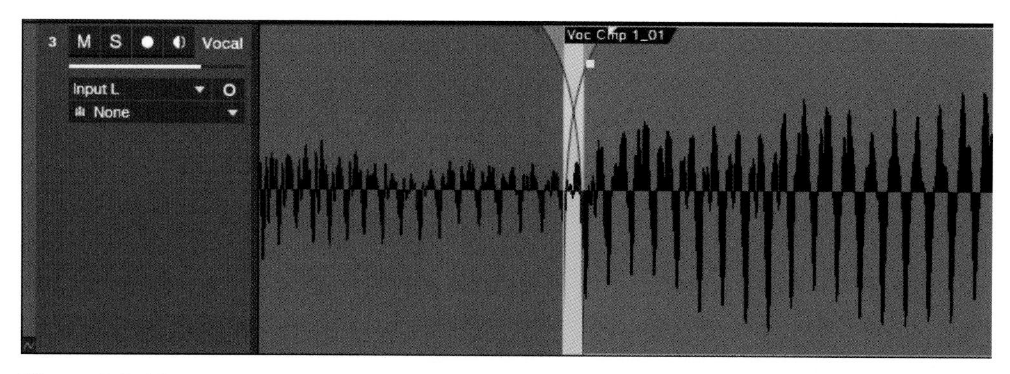

Figure 3.6 The word on the right needed to have a higher level; note the abrupt level change compared to the lower-level word on the left. The split between the two words has a crossfade to smooth out the transition.

Before you commit to this type of phrase-by-phrase editing, listen to any transitions to make sure there's no click or other discontinuity. If there is, you'll need to split at the click, then crossfade the adjoining regions over it as described above. In some cases, fading out just before the click and fading in just after the click will solve any issues with clicks or bad transitions. For these kinds of fades, you're usually best off with a concave (fast) fade curve, because this covers more of the click.

See Figure 3.2 in Chapter 3 of this book for examples of concave fades.

Tech Talk: Phrase-by-Phrase Normalization with Melodyne

Any version of Melodyne above Melodyne essential allows doing phrase-by-phrase normalization. Open up the vocal that needs fixing in Melodyne, and then choose the Percussive algorithm. In this mode, the "blobs" represent individual words or in some cases, phrases. Grab the Amplitude tool and click on a blob. Drag up to raise the level or down to decrease the level to create a smooth vocal line with consistent levels (Fig. 3.7).

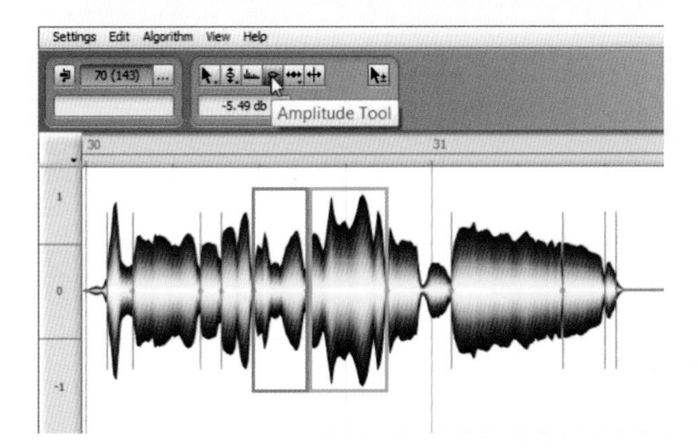

Figure 3.7 Increasing the level of the blob highlighted in blue, and lowering the level of the blob highlighted in green, can bring their levels more into line with the rest of the vocal.

If needed, you can split blobs with Melodyne's split tool to gain more control; for example, you might find that just the ending of a word needs a level increase.

A couple of cautions apply here. First, don't try to increase the levels beyond the available headroom. And second, be aware that some blobs might be a breath inhale or plosive; you don't want to raise those, so listen while you adjust.

Step 5: De-Essing

While a brighter, more trebly vocal can improve articulation, it can also emphasize "s" sounds. Using a de-esser prior to adding other processes can tame these sounds and keep them from being too shrill or prominent.

Reduced to essentials, a de-esser is a simply a compressor that affects only high frequencies. A multiband compressor or dynamic equalizer can perform de-essing, but a dedicated de-esser will usually take less time to adjust.

Dynamic equalization and multiband compression are discussed in Chapters 4 and 5 of this book, respectively.

A de-esser can do more than take care of only high sounds. I recently mixed a song with an overly loud vocal "shh" sound that didn't reach particularly high frequencies; by setting a de-esser to its lowest frequency, I was able to reduce it.

Most de-essers have an option to let you hear only what will be reduced by the de-esser, typically enabled by a switch called something like *listen*, *audition*, or *sidechain*. Other controls let you set the frequency at which the de-essing occurs and the depth of frequency removal. With the listen function enabled, you can sweep the frequency control until you hear the sound you want to minimize, then adjust the depth control for the desired amount of "s" reduction (Fig. 3.8).

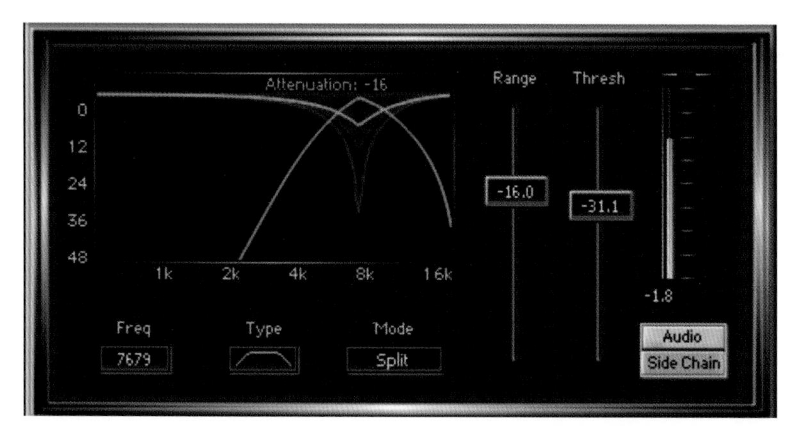

Figure 3.8 The Waves Renaissance DeEsser set to compress frequencies around 8 kHz.

After turning off the listen function, check the vocal in context with the rest of the tracks. You may be surprised to find even a little bit of de-essing sounding too drastic, so reduce the de-essing depth if needed.

Step 6: Pitch Correction

At this point, the vocal should be cleaner, with a more consistent level, and with any annoying artifacts tamed. And you should have been able to do this all without reducing the vocal's natural qualities. With this solid foundation, you can start doing more elaborate processes like pitch correction.

Yes, the critics are right: pitch correction can suck all the life out of vocals by making the pitch inhumanly accurate. I discovered this myself accidentally when working on some background vocals. I wanted them to have an angelic, perfect quality. Because the voices were already very close to proper pitch anyway, I thought just a tiny bit of manual pitch correction would give the desired effect. This proved to be totally wrong. The pitch correction took away what made the vocals interesting—the fact that they *weren't* totally on pitch. It was an epic fail as a sonic experiment, but a valuable lesson. It caused me to start analyzing vocals to learn what makes them interesting, and what pitch correction takes away.

And that's when I found out that the critics are also wrong, because pitch correction—if applied selectively—can enhance vocals tremendously, without anyone ever suspecting the sound had been corrected. Pitch-correcting vocals needn't impart a robotic quality.

The examples here reference Celemony Melodyne, but other programs like Waves Tune, iZotope Nectar, and of course the grand-daddy of them all, Antares Auto-Tune, all work similarly. First they analyze the vocal, after which they display the note pitches graphically against a grid (much like the *piano roll* view for MIDI notes). The vertical axis shows pitch, while the horizontal axis shows time (Fig. 3.9).

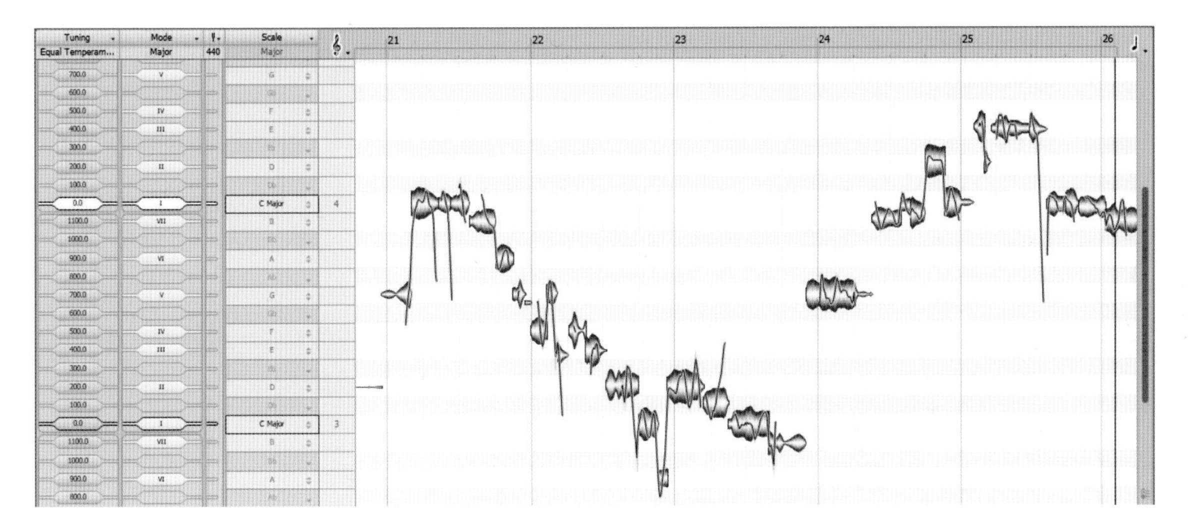

Figure 3.9 Celemony's Melodyne showing an analyzed vocal and individual notes (the "blobs," as Celemony calls them) mapped to pitches. Dragging a blob upward raises pitch; dragging downward lowers pitch.

You can generally quantize the notes to a particular scale with looser or tighter correction, and often correct timing as well as pitch. With most pitch correction software you can also turn off automatic quantizing to a particular scale, and instead correct pitch manually if you want to make more subtle changes.

Pitch correction works best on vocals that have no significant processing. Modulation and time-based effects can make pitch correction glitchy at best and impossible at worst. Even EQ that emphasizes the high frequencies can create unpitched sibilants that confuse pitch correction algorithms. Aside from the level-based DSP processes mentioned previously, the only processing that's "safe" to use on vocals prior to employing pitch correction is de-essing. If your pitch correction processor inserts as a plug-in (such as, iZotope's Nectar), then make sure it precedes any other processors in the signal chain.

Retaining a Natural Sound with Pitch Correction

The key to natural-sounding pitch correction is simple: don't correct anything that doesn't actually sound wrong, because removing a vocal's pitch variations can actually create a less compelling performance. Applying correction selectively instead of automatically takes more effort (and you'll become best friends with your program's Undo button), but the human voice doesn't always work the way pitch correction would like it to work when doing automatic correction.

Nor do you always need to quantize exactly to pitch. Music is about tension and release, and subconsciously, performers will often start a note or passage a little flat or sharp (tension) and resolve it on pitch (release). Making all the pitches "perfect" removes this emotional component. As an analogy, consider B.B. King's guitar playing. He often bent a flatted 7th not quite up to pitch. By not resolving the note, instead of completing the phrase it led you into the next one. Timing and pitch variations are essential parts of music, so don't overdo the correction.

Also be careful not to remove natural slides from one note to another. One of my favorite synth programming tricks on choir and voice presets is to add short, subtle upward or downward pitch shifts at the beginning of phrases. Singers rarely go from no sound to perfectly pitched sound, and the shifts add realism to presets. Pitch correction can have a natural tendency to remove or reduce these shifts, which is partially responsible for pitch-corrected vocals sounding artificial. So, it's crucial not to "correct" slides that contribute to a vocal's urgency (Fig. 3.10).

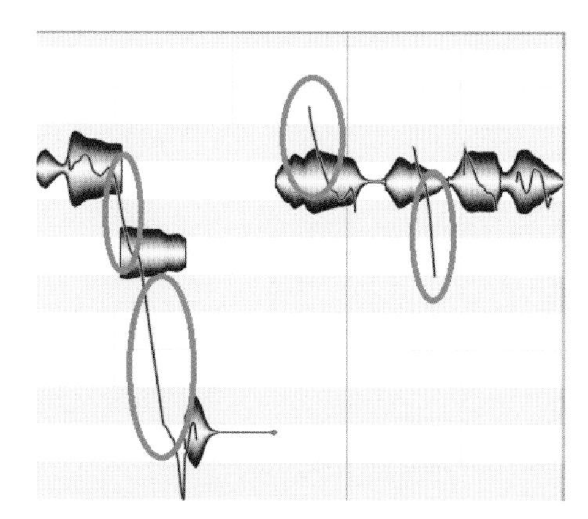

Figure 3.10 Melodyne displays the slides from one note to another (circled in green) as well as the pitch associated with the note.

How Pitch Correction Can Create Vocals with *More* Soul

A common complaint from purists is that pitch correction takes the humanity out of a part—and if overused, it can. But there's a flip side. When I added pitch correction to the arsenal of tools for my own vocals, I found that I became *less* inhibited knowing that if I hit a few bad notes in an otherwise good performance, pitch correction could fix it. I became more likely to stretch my vocals a bit and experiment, rather than being overly concerned about going off-pitch.

Step 7: Tweak the Vibrato

Sometimes a singer's vibrato can run away from the pitch, and the variations become excessive. With Melodyne, the Note Separation tool can help fix this.

Don't assume that the Note Separation tool is not in Melodyne essential because there's no button for it. If you hover the mouse just over the top of a note, the Note Separation tool will appear as a vertical bar cursor with two arrows.

Let's examine how to fix a note with pretty ragged vibrato. First, use the Note Separation tool to separate the blob at each cycle of vibrato. The blobs may change pitch, because Melodyne maps each blob to its average pitch. Cutting a note into smaller blobs defines the average pitch more precisely. (See Fig. 3.11.) If Melodyne corrects a blob to the wrong semitone after you separate the parts, simply drag it up or down a semitone, as appropriate. (The last blob in Figure 3.11 below needs to be brought down a semitone.)

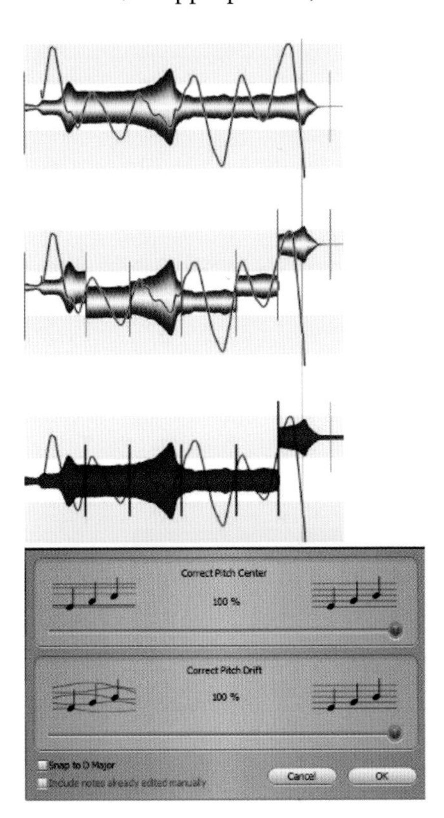

Figure 3.11 The top phrase shows the original vibrato, the middle phrase has cut the vibrato into cycles, and the lower phrase shows how pitch-correcting these slices can produce a smoother, more consistent vibrato that still sounds natural.

You can also use splitting to improve the pitch-correction performance. Vowels are more about carrying pitch than consonants, so you'll get more accurate results if they're separated from the consonants and you correct only the vowels.

Fine-Tuning Vibrato

That's as far as you can go with Melodyne essential, but if you have Melodyne editor, you can call up the Pitch Modulation tool and fine-tune the vibrato depth for greater consistency. Figure 3.12 shows the same phrase as the bottom, corrected phrase in Figure 3.11—but the vibrato has been edited to be much more consistent.

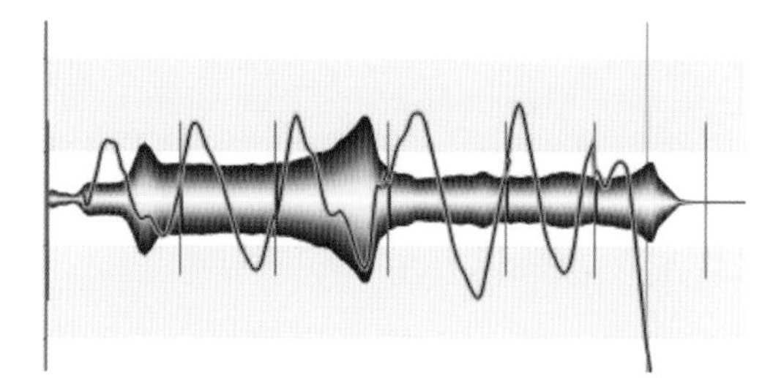

Figure 3.12 You can adjust the amplitude of individual vibrato cycles with Melodyne's Pitch Modulation tool.

Note how the vibrato cycles each have a similar modulation depth in Figure 3.12. And while you may see some discontinuities, you likely won't hear them.

Adding Artificial Vibrato

There's yet another way to add vibrato if a note doesn't have any or if you've flattened pitch variations with pitch correction: use a vibrato plug-in on only certain notes. You can either insert the effect into a clip that contains the part where you want vibrato, or you can split that part off into a separate track and apply a vibrato plug-in. Although the software you use may not have a vibrato processor per se, you can usually use a chorus or flanger to create a vibrato effect (see Fig. 3.13).

Figure 3.13 You can often coax a chorus or flanger into producing vibrato if it includes a mix control that lets you choose 100% processed sound only.

To create vibrato, use only a single voice of flanging or chorusing, set the balance (or mix) to processed sound only, pull way back on the depth (you don't need a lot), and set the rate for the desired vibrato speed. Even better, if the depth is automatable you can fade the vibrato in and out for a more realistic effect. Just remember to keep it subtle, or it will begin to sound fake.

Time to Start Mixing

Once the vocal has been edited to perfection, you can start thinking about the mix. As you play the vocal in context with other tracks, it's time to consider adding signal processing like EQ, dynamics, reverb, and other effects, which we explore in the next few chapters.

For some people, creating effects from scratch using processors can be daunting. Fortunately, presets can provide good starting points. With a little tweaking, presets can often lead to just the results you want. Many plug-ins come with a preset library that demonstrates some of the plug-in's possibilities. If nothing else, you can choose a preset that comes close to the sound you want and then try modifying it to meet your needs.

Some software companies pride themselves on their presets. For example, iZotope's Nectar is a vocal processing plug-in, but one of its main selling points is its large library of presets (see Fig. 3.14).

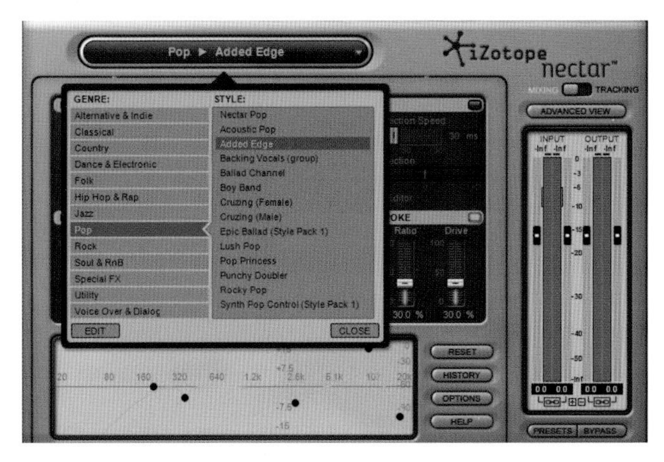

Figure 3.14 iZotope's Nectar combines vocal processing with an extensive library of presets.

However, it's important to remember that presets can take you only so far. Every mic, voice, and mix is different. There is no one-size-fits-all "male vocal" or "female background vocal" preset. A preset that sounds wonderful with a condenser mic might sound terrible with a dynamic mic.

A major value of presets comes into play when you start creating your own, either from scratch or as modifications to existing presets. I've found certain combinations of processors that work well with my voice and the particular microphones I use, so I've saved those combinations as presets. Sometimes one of these presets will work with a piece of music and not require any tweaks. Other times I'll need to make a few changes. But overall, it saves time to have a starting point that has been effective in the past.

Key Takeaways

- After recording your vocal, you can use digital signal processing techniques to prepare the vocal to sit really well in a mix.
- It helps to clean up hiss, handling noise, pops, fades, and other artifacts as much as possible because these can be distracting.
- Consistent vocal levels can have more presence, intimacy, and require less processing. Phrase-by-phrase volume correction is one way to accomplish this.
- For the most natural pitch correction sound, correct only the notes that sound out of pitch.
- You can use pitch correction to improve the consistency of vibrato.

Chapter 4

Equalization

An equalizer emphasizes (boosts) and/or de-emphasizes (cuts) certain frequencies to change a vocal's timbre. The amount of boosting or cutting is expressed in decibels (dB).

Tech Talk: Understanding the decibel

The decibel (dB) is a unit of measurement for audio levels (like an inch or meter is a unit of measurement for length). A 1 dB change is approximately the smallest audio level difference a human can hear. A dB spec can also have a – or + sign to indicate cut or boost. Cutting response in an equalizer band with a setting of –12 dB creates more of a cut than using a setting of –6 dB. A setting of +2 dB would create a slight boost, while a setting of +10 dB would create a major boost.

Equalizer Responses

Equalizers use filter circuits that pass certain frequencies and reject others. The most common filter responses are as follows:

- Low-pass response (Fig. 4.1) passes all frequencies below a certain cutoff frequency (also called a high cut response).

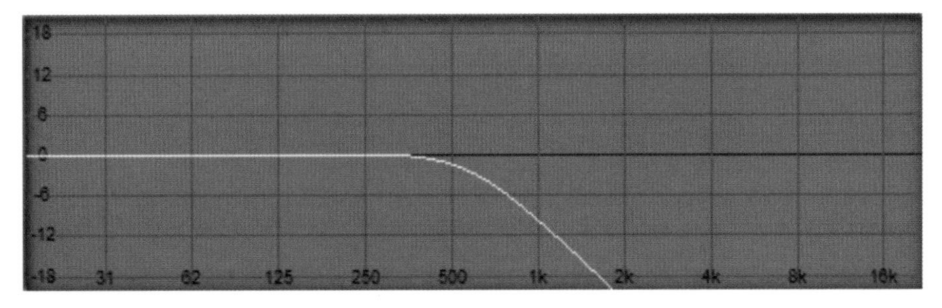

Figure 4.1 Low-pass filter response. The response drops off at higher frequencies.

- High-pass response (Fig. 4.2) passes all frequencies above a particular cutoff frequency (also called low cut response).

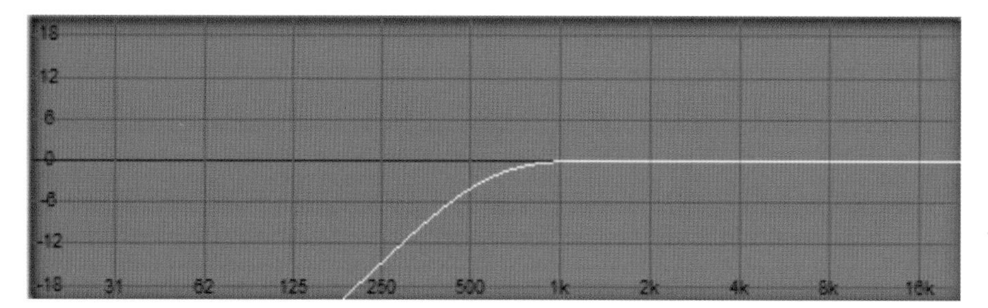

Figure 4.2 High-pass filter response. The response drops off at lower frequencies.

- High-shelf response (Fig. 4.3) starts boosting or cutting the highs at a particular frequency, then levels off to a constant amount of boost or cut.

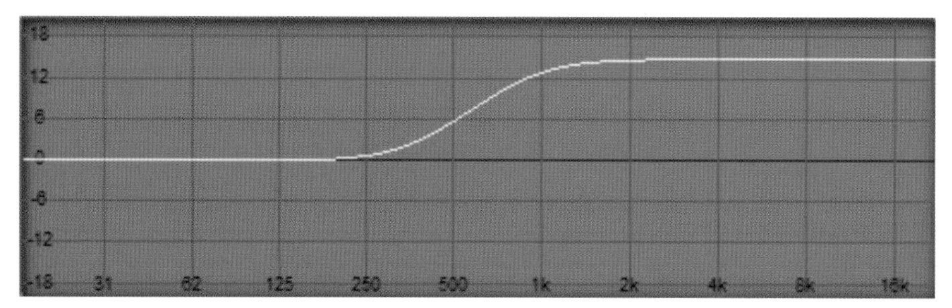

Figure 4.3 This high shelf is boosting the high frequencies.

- Low-shelf response (Fig. 4.4) starts boosting or cutting the lows at a particular frequency, then levels off to a constant amount of boost or cut.

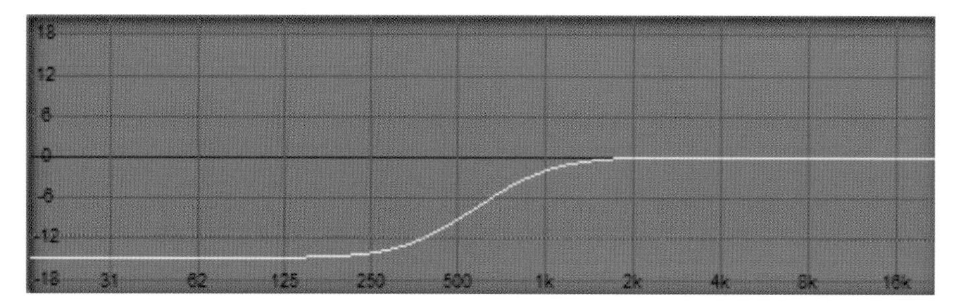

Figure 4.4 This low shelf is cutting the low frequencies.

- Peak/dip or parametric response (Fig. 4.5) boosts or cuts only those frequencies around its resonant frequency, while rejecting higher and lower frequencies. The range of frequencies affected by the peak or dip is called the bandwidth. Peak is also called bandpass or bell, while dip is also called band reject or notch.

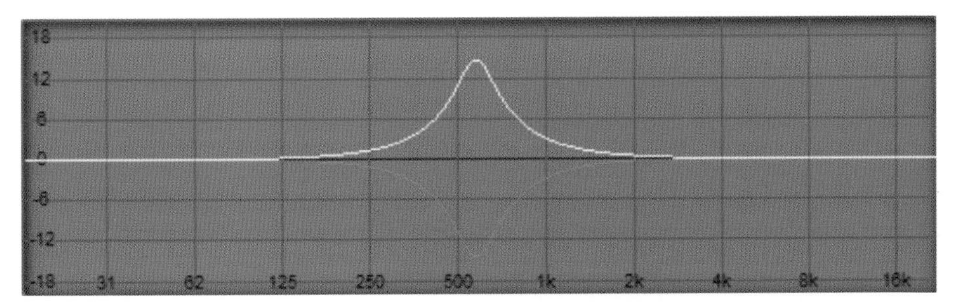

Figure 4.5 Peak/dip filter response. The white curve shows a peak response at a particular frequency, while the orange curve shows the response for an equivalent cut (notch filter) at the same frequency.

Depending on the vocal, all these filter types can have their uses. Common equalizers often include multiple bands and offer different response options. For example, a four-band equalizer might have two parametric (or quasi-parametric) stages, a band that can switch between low shelf or low-pass response, and another band that can switch between high shelf or high-pass response. However this is by no means set in stone—equalizers can have more or fewer bands, and each band may offer only one type of response or multiple types of response.

Quasi-parametric EQ stages include frequency and boost/cut controls, but do not include bandwidth controls.

Main EQ Parameters

There are three main equalizer parameters.

- Frequency sets the specific part of the audio spectrum where the boosting or cutting will occur.
- Boost/cut (peak/dip) determines the amount of equalization that will be applied at the selected frequency.
- Bandwidth, resonance, or Q determines the sharpness of the boosting or cutting action. Narrow bandwidth settings affect a very small part of the audio spectrum, while broad settings target a wider range (see Fig. 4.6). Shelf, high-pass, and low-pass responses may or may not have bandwidth settings.

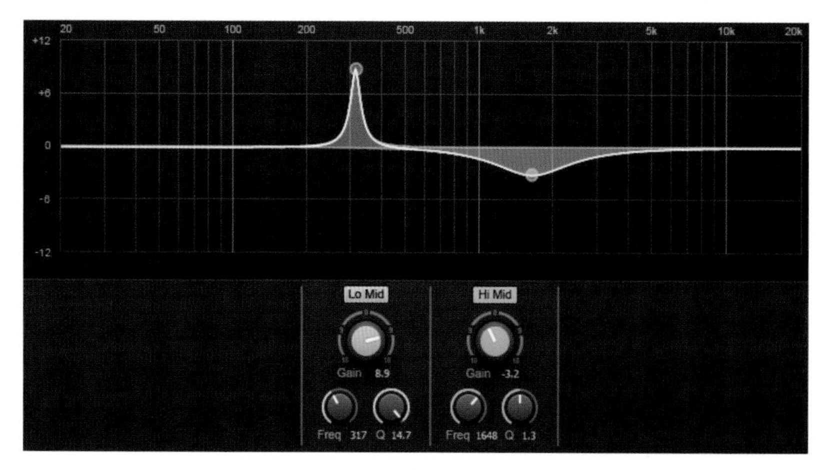

Figure 4.6 The three main parameters of a parametric equalizer. The Lo Mid band (left) is boosting with a narrow Q at 317 Hz, while the Hi Mid band (right) is cutting with a broad Q at 1,648 Hz.

However, one of the most important controls on any equalizer is the bypass switch or button. This lets you compare the unequalized and equalized sounds as a reality check. Use the minimum amount of equalization necessary—just a few dB of change can make a big difference. It's also important to avoid "iterative" EQ re-tweaking, where the lows seem thin so you boost the bass, but now the highs don't seem clear so you boost the highs, and so on. For example, if the vocal sounds thin, instead of boosting the bass try cutting back the highs slightly and raising the overall vocal level.

What You'll End Up Equalizing

Proper equalization helps a vocal sit well in the mix, but the mic itself may already have added the first pass at equalization if it has a natural lift (high-frequency emphasis) in the vocal range. There are three main areas to focus on when applying EQ for the male voice: the low frequencies below about 150 to 200 Hz, upper midrange in the 2 to 4 kHz range, and high frequencies (which can also start in the upper midrange) around 5 to 6 kHz. Use the upper bass and midrange as the reference for vocal EQ—leave that region alone while you work on the lows first, and then the upper midrange and highs.

The male voice can range from about 100 Hz to 500 Hz, while the female voice can cover about 170 Hz to 1000 Hz. You will likely want to raise the filter frequencies mentioned above by several hundred Hz for female vocals.

The Lows

EQ can address excessive bass due to the proximity effect, caused by singing too close to mics with a directional response. However some singers use the proximity effect to sound fuller, so reduce the low end only if it dominates or leads to a muddy or muffled sound. A high-pass filter curve usually works well for this, with a moderate slope (e.g., 6 or 12 dB/octave; see Fig. 4.7).

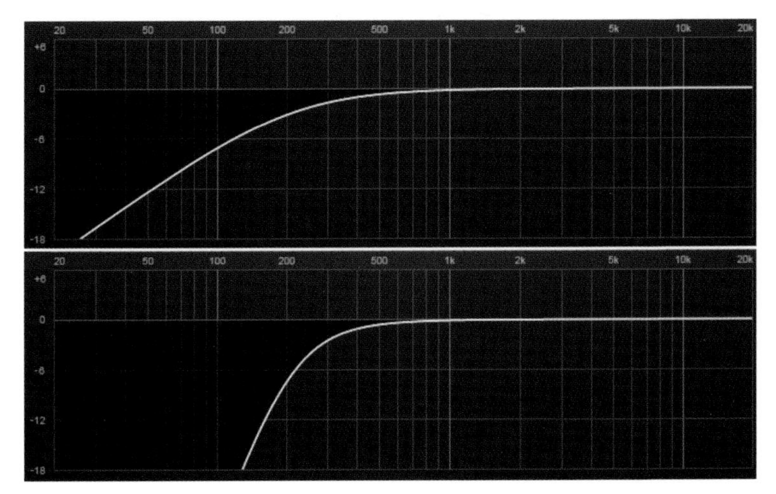

Figure 4.7 The upper curve shows a high-pass filter with a 6 dB/octave slope, while the lower curve shows a high-pass filter at the same frequency but with a steeper, 24 dB/octave slope.

Use looped playback for a section of the vocal where the proximity effect is problematic; then slowly bring up the high-pass cutoff frequency. Strive for the proper balance of low-frequency energy to give a rich, full sound, while not overwhelming the rest of the vocal. If it's difficult to find the "sweet spot"—if the vocal goes from too much bass to not enough—try a gentle 6 dB/octave slope. If the proximity effect is severe, you may need a 24 dB/octave or even steeper slope.

Sometimes reducing the proximity effect's lowest frequencies makes the voice too thin, with no suitable compromise setting. Here a shelving EQ may work better, thanks to a trick many engineers use: Set the shelf frequency and then cut to reduce the muddiness, but add some resonance (Q) to produce a slight bump (level increase) just above the cutoff. (Some high-pass filters allow adding resonance as well, which can be equally or more effective.) This bump increases bass out of the range of the proximity effect, so you can still reduce the lowest frequencies while retaining a relatively full sound.

The Highs

There are two components to the highs. One is the upper midrange, which provides intelligibility (discussed below). The other is the treble range, starting at about 5 to 6 kHz, which gives the vocal air and transparency. A high-frequency shelf with little or no resonance often works well, unless the vocal is hissy or there are "ess" problems that a de-esser can't fix. In that case, apply a parametric boost in the 4 to 7 kHz range instead, with a wide Q. This should give a glossy, intelligible high-frequency response without boosting the ultra-high frequencies.

The Upper Midrange

Listen carefully to the vocal in context with the rest of the mix, because fixing the lows and highs may be all that's needed. Set the vocal's level in relation to the mix so that you can hear the low and high ends clearly. But if the vocal still sits too far back in a busy track, focus on the upper mids with a stage of parametric boost, typically in the 2.5 to 4.5 kHz range. It's not necessarily a problem if this overlaps with the high-frequency shelf—the shelf provides a general boost, while the upper-mid EQ provides a more focused boost.

The human ear is most sensitive in this frequency range. Set a bit of a boost with moderate Q and sweep slowly across the upper mids. There will usually be a frequency where the vocal sounds present and intelligible. Avoid too much boost, because the ear's sensitivity means frequencies in this range can sound harsh. This may also make the lows and highs seem deficient. If the vocal still doesn't seem prominent enough after a conservative upper midrange boost, then you probably need to raise the vocal's overall level.

The Lower Midrange/Upper Bass

One final problem may be too much energy around 300 to 400 Hz. Because many instruments produce energy in this range, the sounds can pile up and get muddy. A slight, somewhat broad cut in this area can tighten up the vocal.

Dynamic Equalization

Dynamic EQ causes equalization to react based on the dynamics of what it's processing. Dynamic EQ specifies a threshold for a particular frequency range. If the audio in that range passes over the threshold, then the EQ either boosts or cuts, depending on which you want.

With a vocalist, this means you could use a static EQ to boost the intelligibility frequencies, but follow this with a stage of dynamic EQ that tames those frequencies if the audio exceeds a certain level. Dynamic EQ is also useful for reducing resonances that aren't a problem at lower levels, but can be annoying if they're too loud. De-essing on vocals is another candidate for dynamic equalization.

Dynamic equalization is more a tool for mastering and solving problems with specific instruments (like taming an overly-bright hi-hat or synthesizer filter), but it can also be useful with vocals.

Automated Equalization

You've heard of self-driving cars... well, we're starting to enter the age of "self-driving audio," where plug-ins use purported artificial intelligence (AI) to aid in the recording, mixing, and mastering process. Currently the approach is fairly basic: the plug-in analyzes your vocal, compares it to a representation of an ideally equalized vocal, then applies changes as needed to more closely match your recording to that ideal vocal.

You can think of automated processing as a way to automate preset creation—instead of hoping that a preset makes up for any deficiencies in your audio, the generated preset has actually analyzed deficiencies in your audio and tried to compensate for it. The most common application of this type of processing is iZotope's Neutron, which is fully editable so you can tweak the automated settings to your liking.

Typical EQ Curves for Vocals

It's common to combine several of these stages—for example, a high frequency shelf that starts boosting around 3 kHz to brighten the vocal, with a slight parametric boost around 3.5 kHz to increase intelligibility, and a slight bass cut to deal with boominess. In this section, I've provided examples of some typical EQ curves for vocal applications. Just remember that these are generalized and sometimes exaggerate settings so that the differences are obvious. You may want to make the parameter values less drastic. Furthermore, every vocalist is different, as is every mic and every musical context.

In these examples, note that individual bands are color-coded, so you can see their response settings. The white band indicates the total result of all the individual bands, and it represents the actual, final EQ that gets applied to a signal.

Male Vocal

This first EQ curve is a common starting point for male vocal EQs: a high shelf boost to add air, a bit of an upper midrange boost to increase intelligibility, a bit of a lower midrange cut, and a resonant high-pass cut. Increasing the high-pass filter's resonance produces a slight bass bump that gives a warmer lower register (see Fig. 4.8).

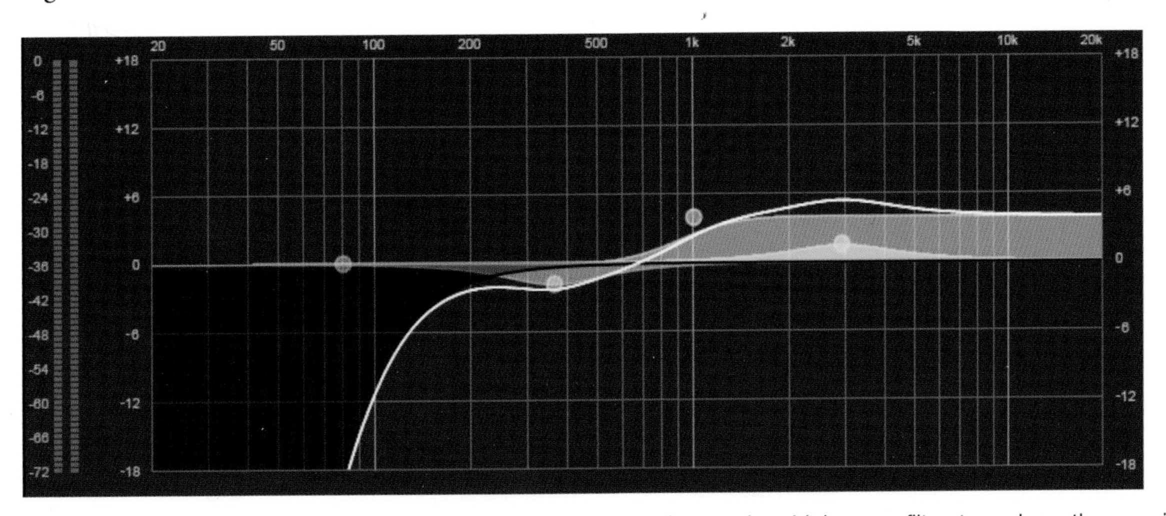

Figure 4.8 This EQ curve applies several tweaks to a male vocal: a high-pass filter to reduce the proximity effect, a high-frequency shelf for air and transparency, an upper mid boost to increase intelligibility so the vocal can stand out more, and a tiny lower midrange dip.

Airy Ahhs

This curve is suitable for airy, choir-type vocals that float above the music. It takes out all the lows, gives a significant high-end lift with shelving, and includes a major midrange cut at 1 kHz so these voices stay out of the range of other vocals and instruments (see Fig. 4.9).

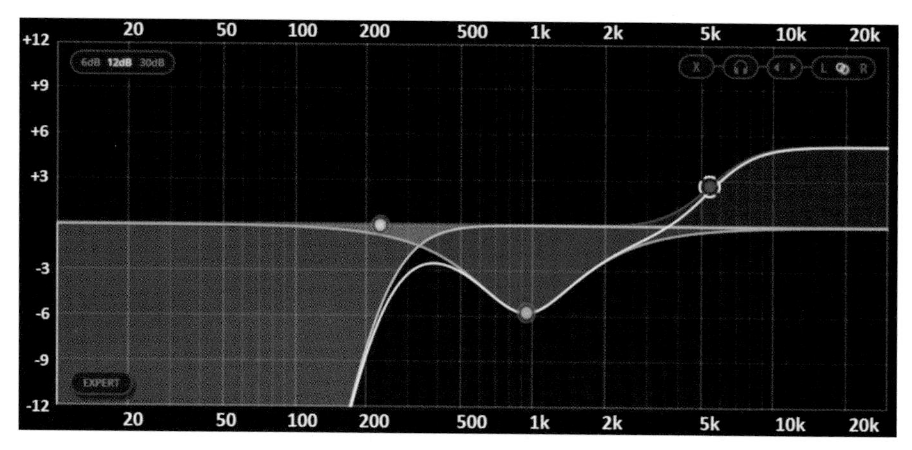

Figure 4.9 Try this curve for angelic, airy "oooh" and "ahhhh" choir sounds.

Ballad Vocals

For ballads, you want a warm, intimate sound, which implies a low-end boost. Of course, singers can do this naturally by taking advantage of a mic's proximity effect, but the vocal you're processing may not have been recorded that way. Meanwhile, the two peaks around 1.6 kHz and 6 kHz maintain intelligibility, while the midrange cut around 500 Hz keeps the low end from being too overbearing (see Fig. 4.10).

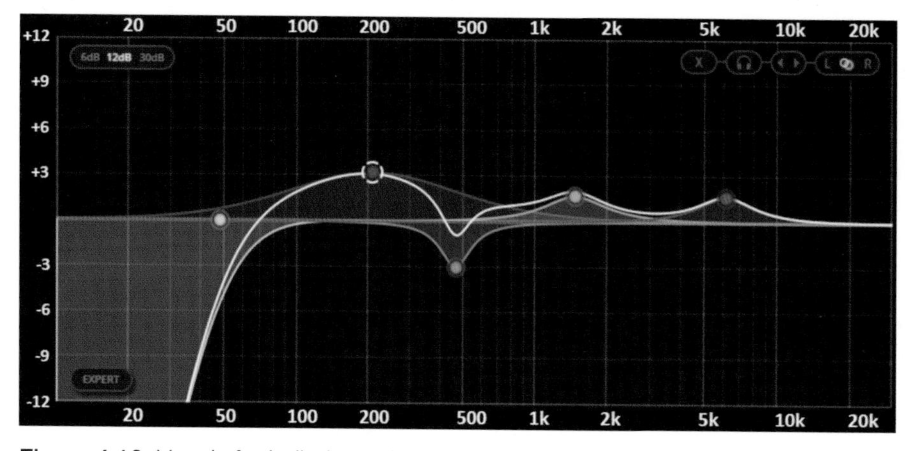

Figure 4.10 Vocals for ballads tend to emphasize warmth.

Dynamic Mic Enhancer

Dynamic mics often sound duller than condenser mics, but some singers prefer the potentially more beefy tone. To add a bit more high frequency sparkle, the high shelf in this example boosts the high end, the high-pass filter minimizes popping and the proximity effect, and the extra peak at 1 kHz gives more intelligibility to the vocals (see Fig. 4.11).

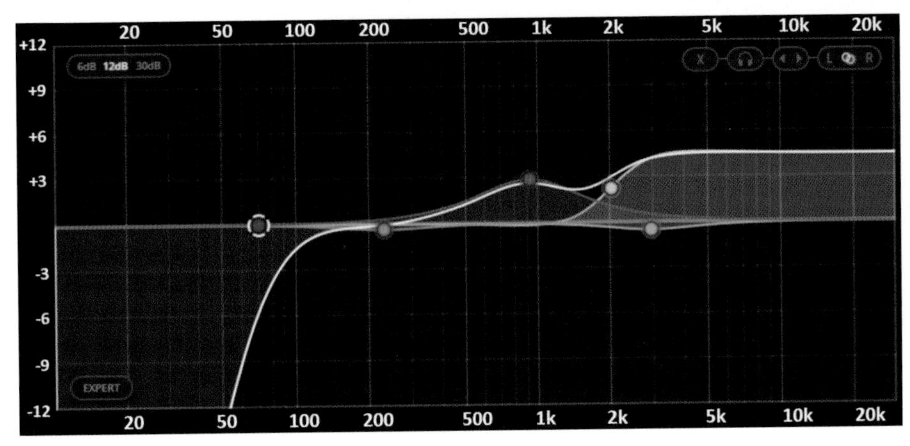

Figure 4.11 This curve can increase intelligibility with dynamic mics.

Podcasting

There's more to recording vocals than singing—like podcasting. Here, intelligibility is crucial. The EQ curve in this example adds plenty of high-end emphasis. There's no real need for extremely high or low frequencies in this application, so they've been removed with a low-pass filter and a high-pass filter, respectively. Note that the width control on each of these filters is turned up quite a bit to give a resonant peak. This curve includes a dip around 400 Hz to reduce mud, and a high shelf to add a treble boost complementing the low-pass filter's resonant peak (see Fig. 4.12).

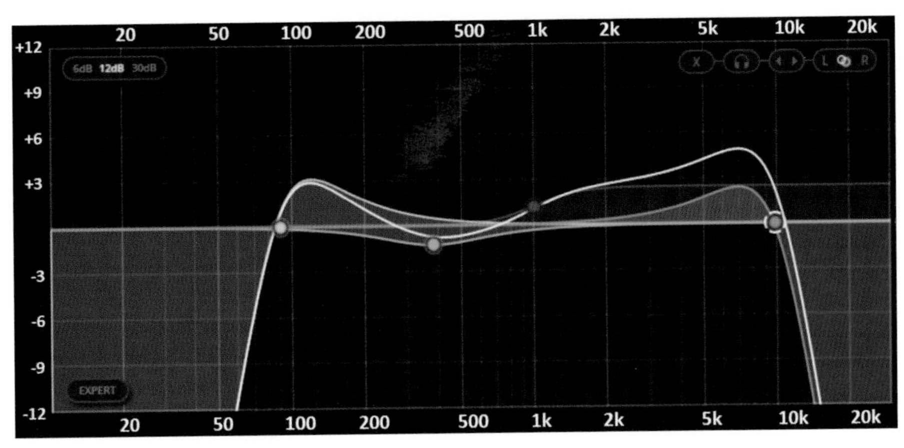

Figure 4.12 Compared to singing, podcasting requires more specialized equalization.

Virtual Pop Filter

If you need to clean up pops after the fact, equalization can come to the rescue. The curve in this example minimizes low frequencies by stacking up six high-pass filters, thus creating an extremely steep slope (see Fig. 4.13).

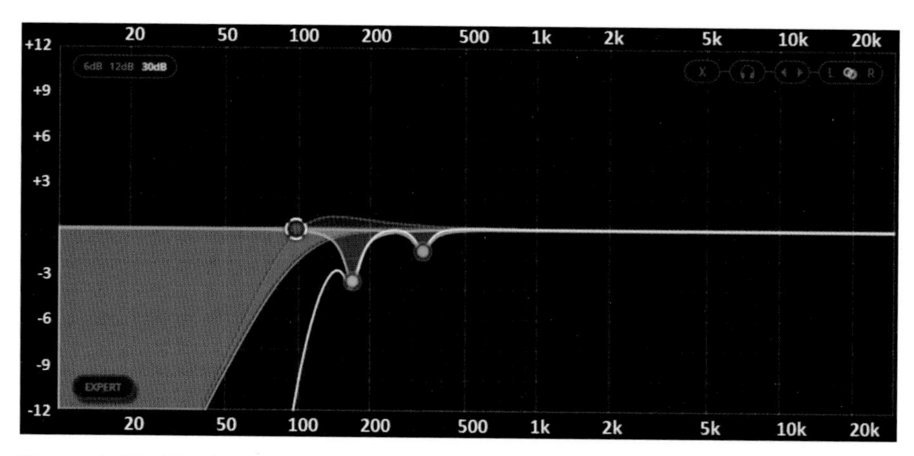

Figure 4.13 Six high-pass filter nodes are stacked on top of each other behind the red node to create a steeper low-frequency cutoff. Two additional nodes reduce other low frequencies.

Key Takeaways

- All types of equalizer responses have their uses for vocals, but the parametric and shelf responses are the most common.
- Reducing low frequencies below the vocal range can tighten the sound and make it more focused.
- Boosting frequencies in the upper midrange increases intelligibility. But don't get carried away, because the ear is most sensitive in this range.
- You can automate EQ if it needs to change dynamically, depending on what's happening in the rest of the mix.
- When using presets, remember they're just starting points. You'll likely need to tweak the parameters.

Chapter 5
Dynamics Processing

Dynamics control is an important part of recording vocals. The best dynamics control is provided by someone who knows good mic technique and plays the mic like a slide trombone—getting closer for more intimate sections and moving further away when singing more forcefully. However, vocalists who have a great command of mic technique are relatively rare, so you may need to use electronic dynamics control instead—and even for vocalists who do have good mic technique, there are some excellent reasons to use it.

Dynamics processing has other uses, like giving a vocal a more intimate feel by bringing up lower-level sounds. No matter what your application, though, don't process the dynamics so much that you also squeeze the life out of the vocals.

How Dynamics Processors Work

Dynamics processors are like invisible hands that alter the gain automatically. For example, to maintain a constant level, if the vocal goes above a certain input level, a compressor will reduce the output level to compensate. Although in theory you could do this manually, an electronic device can react much more precisely and quickly.

Types of Dynamics Processors

The main types of dynamic processors are compressors, limiters, noise gates, and expanders. We'll look at each type and review some tips on how best to use them.

Compressors

The most important compressor controls are the threshold and ratio. When the input goes above the threshold, then compression kicks in to turn down the level. Some compressors have an essentially fixed threshold, so they have an input gain or input control to vary the level going into the compressor. Higher input levels therefore lead to more compression.

Ratio determines how much the output will increase as the input continues to increase beyond the threshold. For example, if the ratio is 2:1, then for a given input level increase, the output level increases by only half as much. In technical terms, an input level increase of 6 dB would allow the output to increase by only 3 dB. If the ratio is infinity, then the output will not increase above the threshold.

To clamp down on peaks while leaving the rest of the vocal dynamics more or less intact, choose a high ratio (10:1 or greater) and a relatively high threshold (around –1 to –6 dB). To compress a wider range of the vocal, use a lower ratio (e.g., 1.5 or 2:1) and a lower threshold, like –15 dB. Lower compression ratios (1.2:1 to 3:1) give a more natural sound than higher ones.

Be careful not to apply too much compression. Our ear/brain combination can differentiate among very fine pitch changes, but not amplitude changes. So, you may have a tendency to overcompress until you can hear the effect, which produces an unnatural sound. Until you've trained your ears to recognize subtle amounts of compression, you can monitor what the compressor is doing by observing the gain reduction meter. This shows how much the input signal's level is being reduced at any given moment. I typically don't want much more than 6 dB of reduction, although some peaks might exceed that. To reduce the amount of gain reduction, either raise the threshold parameter or reduce the compression ratio. Compression naturally reduces the output level, so there will be a gain control to make up for the loss of level (usually called makeup gain, or simply gain). Adjust this control so that the output meter indicator comes close to 0 dB, but never hits or exceeds it. Fig. 5.1 shows some typical plug-in compressors and their associated controls.

Figure 5.1 Several typical compressors

Other Compressor Parameters

The attack time control sets how long it takes for the compression to react after the input exceeds the threshold. An attack time of 0 will clamp down on peaks instantly, producing the most drastic compression action. Use this if it's crucial that the signal never hit 0 dB, yet you want high average levels. But consider using an attack time of 5 to 20 ms to let through some peaks.

A decay (or release) control determines how long it takes for the circuit to stop compressing after the input signal returns below the threshold. This setting is not as critical as the attack: a decay of 100 to 250 ms works well. Note that some compressors can adjust attack and/or decay times automatically, based on the signal passing through the system. This often gives the optimum effect, so try this option before you start experimenting with the attack and release settings.

The knee parameter controls how rapidly any compression kicks in. With a soft knee, when the input exceeds the threshold the compression ratio is less at first, but then increases up to the specified ratio as the input increases. With hard knee response, as soon as the input signal crosses the threshold, it's subject to the specified ratio. Use hard knee settings when controlling peaks is a priority, and soft knee curves (commonly used with vocals) for a less colored sound.

As with equalization, the bypass button is also your friend. You may be surprised to find that even with 6 dB of compression, you don't hear much apparent difference—but bypass the compressor, and you'll hear a change.

Multiband Compression

A multiband compressor splits the incoming signal into multiple frequency bands, and then compresses each band individually. The main benefit is with complex material, like a mix or drum track, so that (for example) a low-frequency kick drum being compressed won't also cause a high-frequency cymbal to be compressed.

Because vocals aren't polyphonic or harmonically complex, multiband compression isn't as relevant. Where it can be useful is for de-essing if you don't have a dedicated de-essing plug-in. For this you would choose a high-frequency or upper-midrange band that covers the "s" sound, and then apply compression to only that range.

Limiters

Limiters are based on compression. The difference is that they have the same intended function as a governor on a motor—if an input signal exceeds a set threshold, the output will not increase (this is like a compression ratio of infinity to 1). In practice, a high compression ratio, like 20:1, is functionally equivalent to limiting.

Whether to use limiting, compression, or both on voice is a matter of taste and context. Here are some suggestions:

- With a "peaky" vocalist, limiting can be a better choice because it tames the peaks but leaves the rest of the dynamic range alone (Fig. 5.2).

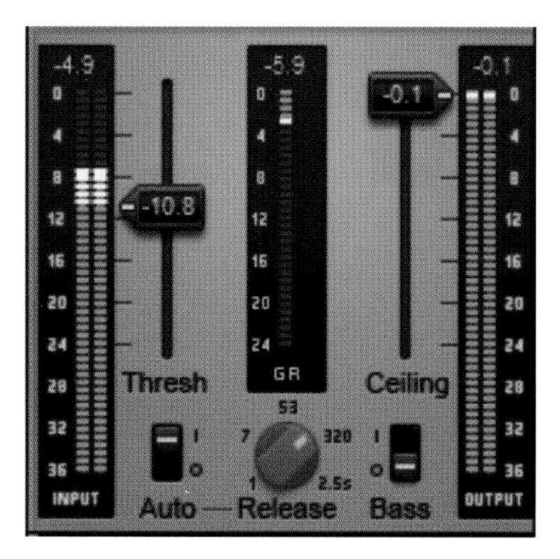

Figure 5.2 A limiter responding to an input level above the threshold. The middle gain reduction (GR) meter shows the amount of reduction being applied to keep the output signal below the output ceiling (set by the right slider).

- If using compression doesn't sound natural (such as when you can hear the compressor working), try using a limiter to control peaks, followed by a compressor set to more conservative settings. Using the limiter means the compressor won't need to do overly drastic compression.
- For transparent compression where you may not even be able to tell any is in use, put two compressors in series, each with a fairly low ratio and relatively high threshold. This tends to round off the effect of the compression. The only drawback is that two compressors may contribute more hiss than a single compressor. However, you won't have to use as much compression with each processor, so there may be no noticeable noise increase.
- If the attack time you want on a compressor allows transients through that cause overloads, consider following the compressor with a limiter whose sole function is to squelch those peaks.

Expanders and Noise Gates

An expander is the opposite of a compressor—below a threshold, the output drops off faster than the input. For example, with an expansion ratio of 1:2, if the input level goes down by 1 dB, the output level drops by 2 dB. The main use with vocals is to set a low threshold, around –45 to –60 dB or so, and use a fairly steep expansion ratio, like 1:4 or 1:10. This will make any low-level noise even quieter, and may eliminate the need to do manual editing to reduce the silence between vocal phrases. With proper parameter settings, the effect can be relatively transparent.

You can also think of an expander as a more refined version of a noise gate, which we met previously in Chapter 3. To refresh, a noise gate mutes the track's audio when the level drops below a user-settable threshold and unmutes the audio when the level goes above the threshold. Because mics are sensitive and preamps are high-gain devices, you may have hiss or other noises when the singer isn't singing. A noise gate can remove these automatically. In fact, expanders are often combined with noise gates, because of the similarity between the two processors—much like how compressors may also include limiting (Fig. 5.3).

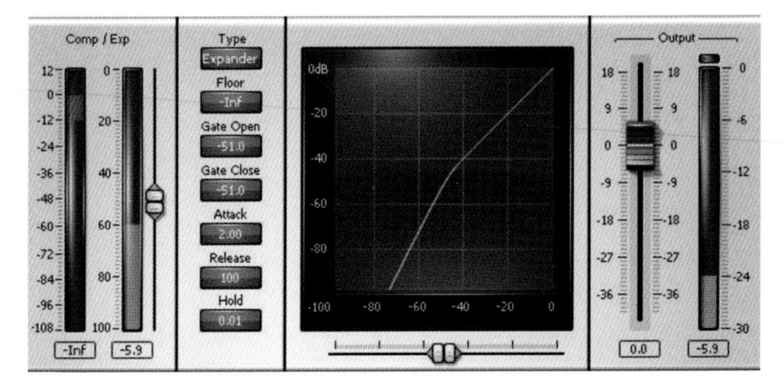

Figure 5.3 The Waves C1 can perform the functions of an expander and a noise gate. It offers several parameters that can tailor the processing to make it less obtrusive.

If the gating action is too abrupt, the voice will sound unnatural. Fortunately, noise gates have controls in addition to threshold that can smooth the gating action. A decay control allows for a smooth transition from the gate being on to off: a typical value is 200 ms. Also, instead of having the audio cut off completely after the gate closes, you'll usually have the option to attenuate by a certain amount so the transition doesn't go to full silence. Try setting attenuation to around 10 dB or so. This will still cut most of the noise, but may sound more natural. In any event, in my experience it can be difficult for noise gates to be completely transparent, which is why I prefer removing spaces between phrases manually.

Sidechaining

Usually, the input signal going into a dynamics processor splits into two paths. One path feeds the input of the audio processor itself, while the other path goes to a separate input that controls the processing. In other words, the control input looks at the signal to determine if it's above or below the threshold, and then adjusts the gain accordingly.

However some compressors, noise gates, and other processors include a feature called sidechaining. This separates the control input, allowing you to feed it with a separate signal. This input is called the sidechain input (see Fig. 5.4).

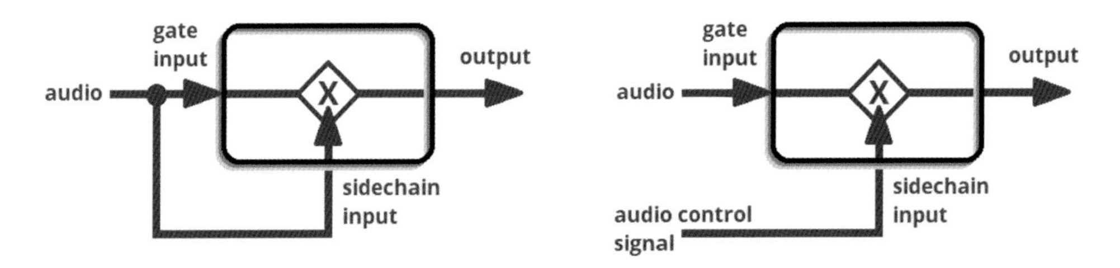

Figure 5.4 The block diagram on the left shows an audio input signal feeding a noise gate and simultaneously controlling the gating action. The diagram on the right shows a different audio signal controlling the noise gate by feeding the sidechain input.

Probably the best way to explain the purpose of sidechaining is with a couple examples. Let's say you're mixing a singer-songwriter project with vocal and guitar, and the guitar is going through a compressor. By splitting the vocal into two paths and sending one to the compressor's sidechain input, the guitar will be compressed (thus lowering the level) whenever the vocalist is singing and the vocal goes above the threshold. When the singer isn't singing, the guitar will return to its normal, uncompressed level.

As a different example, suppose you're mixing background vocals with a percussive genre of music, like electronic dance music or hip-hop. You can set up a noise gate with sidechaining, and then route the vocal through the noise gate. Set the noise gate so that it doesn't fully mute the vocals when closed, but attenuates them by around 6 to 10 dB. By feeding the kick drum into the sidechain input, the vocals will be at a higher level when the kick hits, and a lower level otherwise. This will impart a more percussive vocal effect.

Key Takeaways

- The need to control dynamics is very common with vocals.
- Be careful not to overcompress, because this can produce an unnatural sound. Check the gain reduction meter and use the bypass switch as a reality check.
- The importance of good mic technique cannot be overstated, particularly with directional mics where moving closer to the mic increases the amount of bass.
- Limiters can be very effective with voice and sometimes sound more natural than compression. Try both to discover what works best with your voice.
- Expanders and noise gates can help minimize hiss and other extraneous, low-level sounds. However, having them work transparently is difficult, so it's often necessary to do this kind of work with digital editing as described in Chapter 3.

Chapter 6

Reverb and Delay

Reverb and delay are common effects for enhancing vocals—few recordings put the voice totally out front, with no ambience behind it. We'll start with reverb, because it's such a popular processor, and then look at applications for delay.

Reverb Processing

Recordings are often made in studios where the acoustics are intended to be as dry as possible. You can always add room ambience, but if the room's acoustics are baked into the sound, there's little you can do to remove those characteristics. However, a *totally* dry sound goes against what we expect to hear, because we're used to hearing vocals in some kind of acoustic space, like a concert hall, auditorium, or the like. Reverb's purpose is to create a suitable ambience.

The Different Reverb Types: Which One for You?

Acoustic spaces create the most natural reverb, but there's only one "preset"—and try fitting a concert hall in your project studio! Granted, some people run mics and speakers to a tiled room (e.g., bathroom) for some decent, tight-sounding reverbs. But emulating the classic concrete room sound that was on so many great recordings, let alone other acoustic environments, is not an easy task.

Synthesized Reverb

Synthesized digital reverb (also called algorithmic reverb) ruled the digital reverb world pretty much by itself for several decades. This type of reverb recreates a reverb effect with three processes. The first is *pre-delay,* which emulates the time it takes for a signal to travel from the source to the first reflective surfaces. The second is *early reflections,* the initial sound that happens when sound waves first bounce off of various surfaces. Then comes the reverb *decay*, which is the wash of sound caused by the myriad reflections that occur in a real room, with their various amplitude and frequency response variations (see Fig. 6.1).

Most synthetic reverbs also create diffusion (covered later), which determines whether the echoes are more blended or discrete.

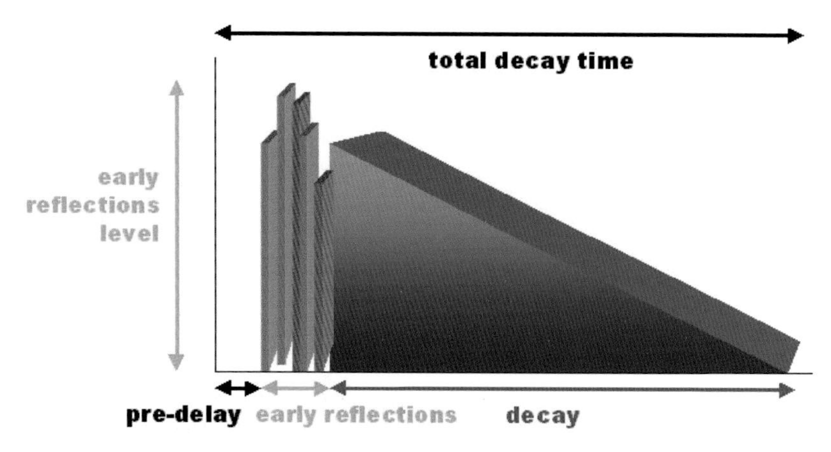

Figure 6.1 Synthesized reverb deconstructs reverb into these parameters.

Many, if not most, digital reverbs are not true stereo devices; they mix stereo inputs into mono, and synthesize a stereo space. This is why you can obtain stereo reverb effects with a mono signal like voice.

Convolution Reverb

You can think of convolution reverb as the equivalent of an audio snapshot of an acoustic space's characteristics, which is then imparted on to your audio. Consider the convolution reverb's impulse as the "mold" of a particular space; the sound is then "poured" into that mold. If the space is a concert hall, then the sound takes on the characteristics of the concert hall. This produces a highly realistic sound, much like a keyboard sampler can produce more realistic sounds than a keyboard synthesizer.

The tradeoff has traditionally been the usual sampler versus synthesizer issue: it can be difficult to edit the sounds. However, many modern convolution reverbs are quite editable and as easy to use as standard reverbs. You may find that changing parameters feels a little slow due to all the calculations being performed, but this isn't a big deal. Thanks to today's faster processors, convolution reverbs have become commonplace. Choosing whether to use convolution or synthesized reverb for voice is a matter of taste (Fig. 6.2).

Figure 6.2 The reverb on the left is Studio One's Open Air reverb, while the reverb on the right is the algorithmic Room Reverb.

Synthesized reverb can give a more diaphanous, airy type of sound, while convolution gives a more realistic, you-are-there kind of vibe. It's kind of like the difference between an impressionistic painting and a photograph; both can give enjoyment, for different reasons.

One Reverb or Many?

Back in the stone age of recording, a mix had one reverb, and all signals were bussed to it. The vocals usually sent more signal than some of the other instruments, but the result was a cohesive group sound.

Later on, studios often used a specific reverb for vocals. Much of the motivation for doing this was to make the voice more distinctive, and if the studio had a *plate reverb* (an early type of mechanical reverb), that was often the reverb of choice because it tended to have a brighter, crisper sound than a traditional room reverb. This complemented the human voice well, which tends not to have a lot of high-frequency response.

The advent of digital reverb allowed people to go a bit crazy—one reverb type on the voice, gated reverb on drums, some gauzy reverb on guitars, and maybe even one or two different reverbs in an aux bus. The result was often a sound that bore no resemblance to the real world. That in itself is not always a bad thing, but if taken to extremes, your ears—which know what acoustical spaces sound like—will recognize the sound as artificial. Unless you're going for a novelty effect, this can be a problem.

If your digital reverb has a convincing plate algorithm, try that as a channel insert effect on vocals, and use a good room or hall reverb in an aux bus for your other signals. To help create a smoother blend, send some of the vocal reverb to the main reverb. This will likely require dialing back the dedicated vocal track reverb level a bit, because the main reverb will bring up the vocal reverb level somewhat (see Fig. 6.3).

Figure 6.3 This mixer routing in Pro Tools shows a Universal Audio EMT 140 plate reverb inserted in the vocal path, along with a send (the white button marked "verb") going to the main hall reverb with the other instruments.

How About a Real Acoustic Space?

Although digital reverbs have made tremendous progress since they were first introduced, there's nothing quite like a physical acoustic space to give an ambient quality that remains elusive to recreate digitally.

But this doesn't mean you need a concert hall to obtain a good reverb sound. Even relatively small spaces, if they're reflective enough, will do the job. Simply send an aux bus out to a speaker in your bathroom (remove any towels or soft surfaces, and pull shower curtains back). Then put a mic in the bathroom and bring its signal back into a mixer input.

Send some of your vocal channel's digital reverb output through an aux bus into this space, and add just enough of the acoustical reverb to provide the equivalent of "sonic caulking" to the digital reverb sound. The room will add early reflections that will be far more complex and interesting than all but the very best digital reverbs can deliver—and you might be very surprised just how much this can sweeten up the sound.

And if you're in an experimental frame of mind, consider adding some feedback to the room reverb. Send some of the room reverb return back into the send output feeding the speaker. Be very careful, though, and keep the monitors at extremely low levels as you experiment—you *don't* want a major feedback blast.

Reverb Parameters and Controls

A sophisticated reverb will have many parameters, and it's not always obvious how to optimize these parameters for specific recording situations. So, let's discuss how the various parameters affect your vocals.

Early Reflections

This is also called initial reflections, and any associated parameters control the time between when a sound occurs and when those sound waves hit walls, ceilings, etc. These reflections tend to be more defined and sound more like discrete echoes than reverb. The early reflections time is usually variable from 0 to around 100 ms, and there will also be a level control to set a balance with the overall reverb decay. Increase the time to give the feeling of a bigger space. For example, if you've dialed in a large room size, you'll probably want to add a reasonable amount of pre-delay as well.

With vocals, I tend not to use a lot of early reflections or pre-delay, because I want the vocal to be upfront. The reverb decay (see next) fills in the background. As usual, this is subjective, so choose the sound that works best for you.

Decay Time and Decay Time Frequencies

Decay is the sound created by the reflections as they continue to bounce around a space. This *wash* of sound is what most people associate with reverb, and is often called the reverb tail. The decay time parameter determines how long it takes for the reflections to run out of energy. Note that long reverb times may sound impressive on instruments when soloed, but they rarely work in an ensemble context (unless the arrangement is very sparse).

Many reverbs offer a *crossover frequency,* which divides the reverb into high and low frequency ranges. This lets you specify separate decay times (abbreviated RT) for high and low frequencies. To prevent too much competition with midrange instruments, consider using less decay on the lower frequencies and more decay on the highs. This adds air to the vocals and also emphasizes some of the sibilants and mouth noises that humanize a vocal. Vary the crossover setting to determine what works best for a particular voice (see Fig. 6.4).

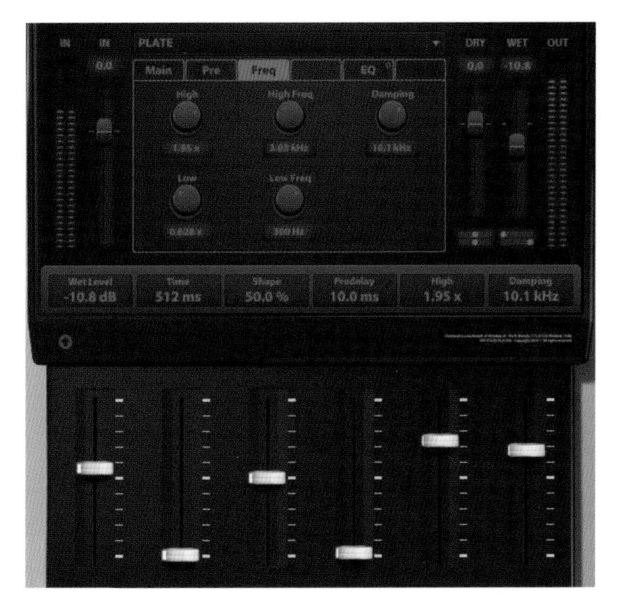

Figure 6.4 The Breverb reverb from Overloud has separate decay times and programmable frequencies for the high and low bands.

Remember that crispness with vocals is usually a good thing, because it increases intelligibility—as long as you didn't already add massive amounts of high frequency EQ to the vocal itself. In any event, experimentation is key to finding the right crossover point because of differences between male and female voices, tonality, range, etc. Start around 1 kHz and move upward from there until you dial in the right sound.

If your reverb sounds overly metallic, try reducing the highs starting at 4 to 8 kHz. Note that many of the great-sounding plate reverbs didn't have much response above 5 kHz, so don't worry if your reverb doesn't provide high frequency brilliance—it's not crucial. Reducing low frequencies going into the reverb reduces muddiness; try attenuating below 100 to 200 Hz.

All these controls have a major effect on the overall reverb character. Increasing the low-frequency decay creates a bigger, more massive sound. Increasing high-frequency decay gives a more ethereal effect. With few exceptions, this is not the way high-frequency sounds work in nature, but an extended high-frequency decay can sound very good on vocals, because in addition to adding more reverb to sibilants and fricatives, it minimizes reverb on plosives and lower vocal ranges. This avoids a boomy reverberation effect; you never want reverb to compete with the vocals.

Diffusion

A reverb's diffusion control increases the density (or thickness) of the echoes. High diffusion places echoes closer together, while low diffusion spreads them out. With percussive sounds, low diffusion creates lots of tightly spaced attacks, like marbles hitting steel. But with voice, which is more sustained, low diffusion gives plenty of reverb effect without overwhelming the vocal from excessive reflections. Because using high diffusion settings can produce a thick reverb sound, there's always the risk that the reverb could overwhelm the voice. Low diffusion settings produce a reverb sound that blends in with the vocals rather than sounding like a separate effect that lives apart from the voice (see Fig. 6.5).

Figure 6.5 Low diffusion settings, as shown here in the Waves Renaissance Reverberator, are often—but not always—preferable for vocals compared to high diffusion settings.

However, with less complex material, you might want more diffusion on the vocals to make the sound richer—plate reverbs were always popular with vocals because of their high diffusion characteristics. As always, the only rule is to obey your ears.

Reverb Algorithm

With synthesized reverbs, the *algorithm* is a fancy name for the type of space being emulated. Typical algorithms synthesize halls, rooms, vintage synthetic reverbs, cathedrals, gymnasiums, closets—anything is possible. There are even reverse reverb algorithms where the decay builds up from nothing to full volume rather than decaying from full volume to nothing, and gated reverb algorithms that cut off the reverb tail abruptly below a certain level (this effect was very popular in the 80s on drums). You probably wouldn't use these on voice except as a novelty-oriented special effect. Most vocals will use a hall or plate algorithm.

With convolution reverbs, the equivalent concept is called an *impulse.* Impulses can capture the sound of specific rooms (like particular concert halls or recording studio rooms). It's also possible to create impulses of older hardware reverbs.

Room Size

This affects whether the paths the waves take while bouncing around in the virtual room are long or short. Just like real rooms, artificial rooms can have resonances and some frequencies where the reflections cancel or add to each other. If the reverb sound has excessive *flutter* (a periodic warbling effect), vary this parameter in conjunction with decay time (described above) for the smoothest sound.

Damping

If sounds bounce around in a hall with hard surfaces, the reverb's decay will be bright and present. With softer surfaces (such as wood instead of concrete, or a hall filled with people), the reverb tails will lose high frequencies as they bounce around, producing a warmer sound. If your reverb can't create a smooth-sounding high end, introduce some damping to place the focus more on the midrange and lower frequencies.

Delay Processing

Adding delay (echo) to voice has been popular since the days of adding slapback echo from a tape recorder. Even subtle amounts of delay can help fill out a vocal and give a bigger sound, without any of the potential drawbacks of doubling the voice.

Delay Parameters

Three main parameters are associated with delay effects: the delay time, the feedback amount, and the wet/dry mix.

Delay Time

This parameter determines the amount of time between receiving the input signal and generating the first echo. With multiple successive echoes, delay time also represents the time difference between subsequent echoes. You'll be able to dial in a specific delay time, like 300 milliseconds. Most modern delay plug-ins also include an option that allows you to sync the delay time to your host program's tempo (Fig. 6.6).

Figure 6.6 Most delay plug-ins allow synchronizing echo time to tempo. In this example, the Sync switch is on (left side of the plug-in display), and the Echo Delay readout shows 1/8 note (middle of the plug-in display).

Older delay units may not include a sync-to-tempo option, but you can calculate the amount of delay for a particular tempo. Use the formula **60,000 ÷ tempo (in BPM) = quarter note delay time (in milliseconds)**. For example, if you wanted a quarter-note delay at a tempo of 95 BPM, you'd set the delay time to 60,000 ÷ 95 = 631.6 milliseconds.

An eighth-note delay is good for thickening vocals; normally you'll mix the echo level fairly low—just enough to reinforce the vocal.

Feedback

This parameter, also called *recirculation*, creates multiple echoes by feeding the output back into the input. When the echo hits the input, it gets delayed and creates another echo. If EQ is included in the feedback path, the timbre of successive echoes can change over time. For example if the feedback path shaves off some high frequencies, then each successive echo will sound less bright than the previous one.

Mix

This parameter sets the balance between the echoes and the original, unprocessed signal. When inserting echo in an auxiliary bus, the Mix parameter is usually set at 100% wet. This is because the main channel fader for the audio source will provide the unprocessed sound, and the two signals can be blended using their respective fader levels.

Other Delay Features

Like everything else in the world of recording, manufacturers are always trying to come up with compelling new delay features to convince you to part with your disposable income. Here are the most common ones.

Tapped Delay

A unit can have multiple delays, each with independent delay times, mix, feedback, panning, etc. This allows setting up complex delay patterns, including polyrhythmic delay effects.

Delay Mode

This usually determines how echoes are placed in the stereo field. In ping-pong mode, successive echoes alternate between the left and right channels. In LCR mode, successive echoes route to the left, center, and right before repeating the pattern.

Modulation

This adds slight variations to the delay time, which can create an effect somewhat like electronic chorusing. It's generally not used much with vocals because double-tracking a vocal, which resembles chorusing but sounds less artificial, is such a common technique.

Tape Echo Emulation

Tape echo, being mechanical, wasn't perfect—there could be a slight flutter, and if the tape heads weren't maintained, the frequency response could be dull. Tape also tended to boost low frequencies and had hiss. Today's plug-ins can emulate these effects to create a vintage sound.

Equalization

In addition to using EQ in the feedback path, note that EQ in general can be your friend when using echo. Some plug-ins include EQ because, for example, rolling off the lows going into the delay (or coming out of it) will help prevent the vocal echo from stepping on the midrange-oriented instruments.

If no EQ is included in the plug-in itself, you can use a send, insert a filter in the send after or before the echo, set the echo for delayed sound only, and then mix in the desired amount of echo to the main signal (see Fig. 6.7).

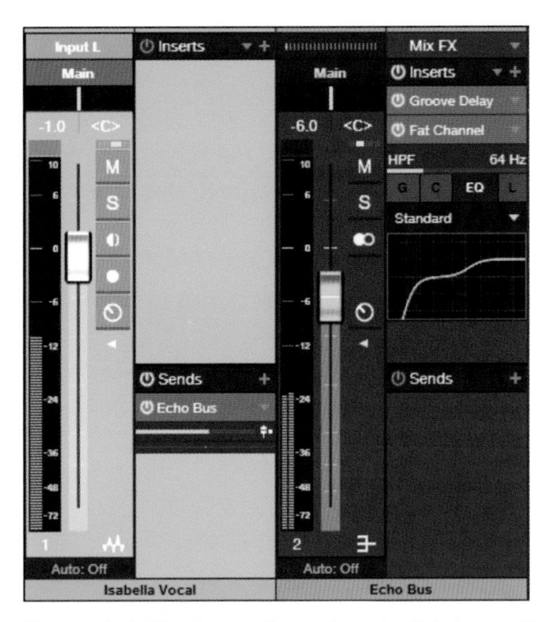

Figure 6.7 The input channel on the left is sending some of its signal to the Echo Bus on the right. An EQ with a high-frequency boost and low-frequency cut follows a delay to shape its response.

Using Delay to Create Long, Trailing Echoes

With this effect, the echo trails off over time to provide a spacey, evocative delay. This is very popular in dance music, with the delay time synchronized to the tempo.

When used more as an effect than for thickening, the echo will likely be mixed higher, have a longer delay time, and include a significant amount of feedback to extend the trail of echoes. This can interfere with the vocal being delayed, which is not necessarily a good thing. To have the echo occur only when you want (such as at the end of a phrase), one possibility is to use automation to apply echo selectively.

Automation is discussed in Chapter 7 of this book.

Here are four possible options for applying delay effects selectively.

Send Effect Bus Automation

One common method is to automate a send to an echo during the sections where you want to introduce the echo. You can automate the echo level or send bus output fader to mix in the desired amount of echo.

Split the Section to Be Echoed to Another Track

By splitting the section to be echoed onto its own track, you may not have to use automation. Instead, you can just set up the echo as a track plug-in. It will affect only the parts of the vocal that you move to that track.

Plug-In Automation

It is also possible to manipulate the desired plug-in controls directly (mainly feedback and mix), and record those changes as automation. This will create automation envelopes that you can manipulate further if needed.

Clip Effects

Some programs let you insert effects in individual clips, not just across an entire track. In this case, you can split the section of a clip where you want to add echo and insert the echo effect in the clip. Note that the echo will not extend beyond the clip boundaries. This will work to your advantage if the clip is followed by a section where you don't want any echo. But for echo effects that require sustain, you may need to extend the clip with silence.

Key Takeaways

- It's rare to hear recorded music where the vocal doesn't have at least some reverb.
- Algorithmic and convolution reverbs provide very different effects. Try both to determine which option flatters your voice the best.
- In most cases, you don't want a lot of low-frequency reverb with voice. Reverb on the vocal's higher frequencies is more common.
- Voices with sustained notes can often benefit from low diffusion reverb settings; too much diffusion may produce a "thick" reverb sound that competes with the vocal.
- Delay (echo) is another common vocal effect.
- Synchronizing delay times to tempo is common in modern productions.

Chapter 7

Automating Parameter Changes

Ideally, the singer will give a perfect performance and all the vocal levels will be perfectly balanced with the rest of the music. However, it's likely that your actual results will fall somewhat short of ideal and you'll want to increase the vocal level in some places and reduce it in others. You might also have situations where you want to change the EQ or some other effect as needed. Fortunately, after you configure levels, panning, or effects settings, you're not locked into them—you can automate parameter changes. This involves either turning knobs while the program records your moves, or programming automation to vary the parameters.

Memorizing fader moves is the classic automation application. For example, if you pull down a vocal track's fader to reduce the level while automating, the software will remember this move and play it back every time you hit that section of the song. When you set the program to read automation, any controls will move as if by magic—which, let's face it, looks pretty cool.

Furthermore, individual clips (isolated pieces of audio within a track) can have clip automation envelopes that are independent of the track. For example, you might want to add a radical stuttering effect to a clip through clip automation, but have it fade out over a time specified by the track automation. Also, you can automate parameters for many signal processing plug-ins, although the specifics depend on the way the plug-in was designed.

Automation Basics

Recording automation moves is a different process compared to recording audio or MIDI data. With most programs, you don't need (or want) the transport to be in record mode. This lets you record automation without being concerned about overwriting recorded audio or MIDI data.

Different programs have different ways of enabling a parameter for automation, so consult your documentation for the details. A common approach is to right-click on a control (or Control-click with a Mac), and select a context menu choice that specifies arming for automation.

Recording programs generally allow you to display automation moves as a line that represents the value of the parameter being automated. This line is called an envelope and can usually be displayed in its own lane (like a subset of a track), superimposed on the track itself, or both.

At the start of a project, a parameter's envelope will either pre-exist as a straight line or will need to be created. Clicking on this line creates a node, which you can then drag higher or lower to change the parameter value, or drag left or right to place its position on the timeline. With enough nodes, you can draw very detailed automation moves. Also, you can often alter the shape of the line between nodes to different types of curves (Fig. 7.1).

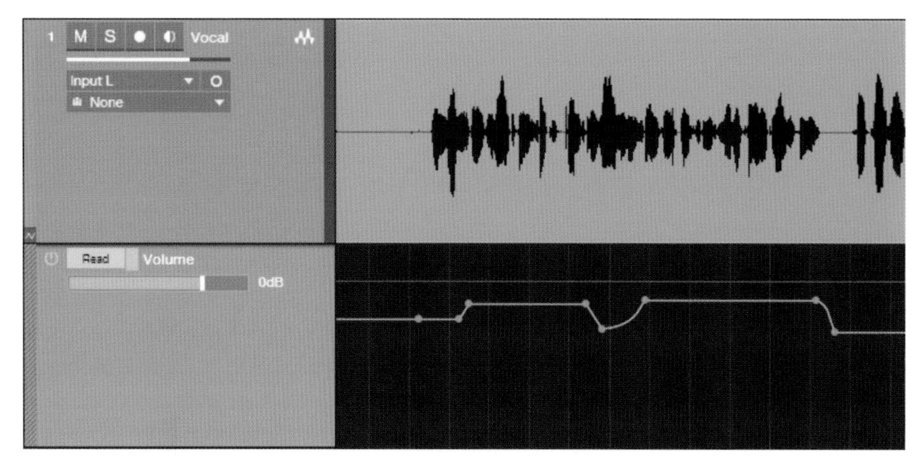

Figure 7.1 The blue line beneath the waveform changes the vocal's volume. The automation is in Read mode, so the envelope will control the level and move the fader automatically.

Automation Methods

There are five main automation methods available in most recording programs.

Method 1: Recording On-Screen Control Changes

This type of automation accommodates the human touch; you can work intuitively by simply moving a fader or other control as desired. (You also have the advantage of being able to edit your moves if touchups are needed.) Although you're limited to moving one parameter at a time when using a mouse, if you invest in a control surface, you can move multiple parameters at a time, like the levels for a vocal and an associated harmony line.

The most common way to record control changes as automation is similar for different programs. Simply enable automation recording, click on the parameter you want to control, and while holding down the mouse button, move the control. To stop writing automation, release the mouse button and/or stop the transport. Any existing automation data will play back in that section.

You can punch in automation over existing automation. Some programs also include a *latch* mode so that when you release the mouse button, the automation value remains the same until changed, instead of reverting to any previous automation data.

To resume recording automation moves, click on a control with the mouse again while the transport is in play mode. This makes it easy to touch up certain parts of the automation while leaving other parts alone.

Method 2: Using Automation Envelope Control

Moving an on-screen control while recording automation creates a corresponding automation envelope. You can edit an existing envelope or draw a new one from scratch, as well as show, hide, copy, paste, and perform other automation-related operations.

Because moving controls creates envelopes, and drawing envelopes moves the on-screen controls they affect, these options are somewhat interchangeable. The method to use depends on the application. For simple level changes, recording control changes is probably the best way to go; but if you want to sync changes to the beat, the envelope approach lets you create more precise automation because you can usually snap envelope nodes to a rhythmic grid (see Fig. 7.2).

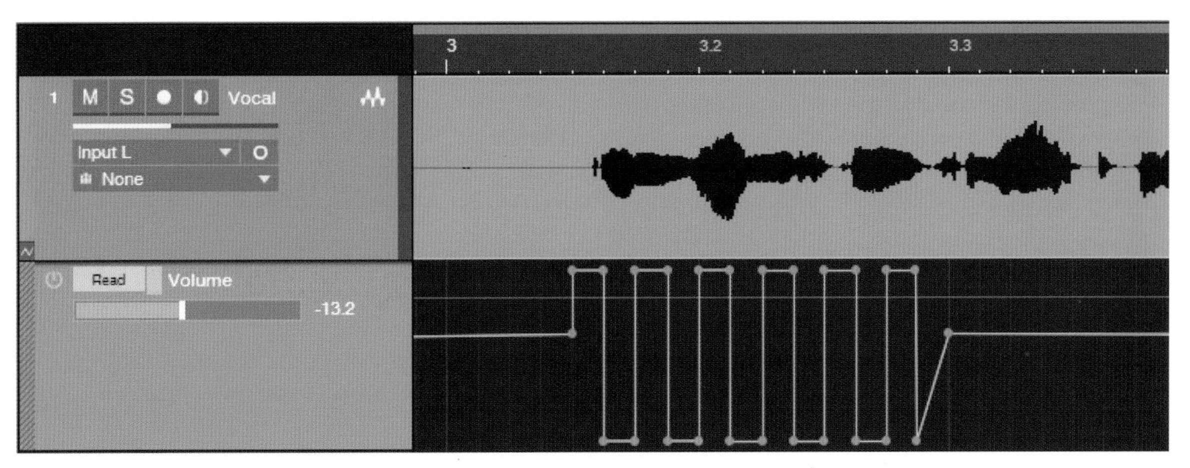

Figure 7.2 This volume envelope creates a stuttering effect by fluctuating rapidly between maximum and minimum level. Snapping the changes to 1/32 notes results in a highly rhythmic effect.

In addition to creating nodes to specify different aspects of an automation envelope, different programs will have ways to move all nodes at once, delete one or more nodes, adjust the line between two nodes, and the like. You'll need to look at your host program's documentation to find the precise functionality your program offers.

Note that clip automation almost always uses envelope control. You may be able to place nodes within the clip, or with simpler methods, have nodes only at the clip's start and end.

Method 3: Recording Automation Moves from a Control Surface

Using an external, hardware control surface for automation follows the same basic procedure as recording a control's on-screen motion, because the control surface mirrors the on-screen faders it controls. Therefore, after setting up a parameter to respond to an external control signal, simply start automation recording and move your hardware faders or knobs/encoders. The data will appear as automation envelopes—just as if you'd moved on-screen controls.

Tech Talk: Control Surfaces

A control surface consists of hardware controls that you can assign to parameters in your host program (or that come pre-assigned). (See Fig. 7.3.)

Figure 7.3 The PreSonus FaderPort 8 provides eight faders as well as multiple switches. While designed to integrate with the company's Studio One recording software, it's universal enough to work with other programs.

Typically, a control surface will have eight faders that map to track level faders, eight knobs (or encoders) that map to track pan pots, mute and solo switches that control the track mute and solo buttons, and record-arm buttons for each track. However, this is by no means a standard—a control surface could be as simple as a single fader, or as complex as something that looks like an old-school mixing console. Some programs include templates for popular control surfaces. This allows for plug-and-play operation: choose the template and all the controls map automatically to the correct parameters. Other control surfaces require that you do the mapping and make assignments yourself.

External control surfaces often have a feature called *touch faders.* This makes it possible to begin recording automation whenever you touch a fader and stop recording when you let go of the fader.

Method 4: Using Snapshot Automation

Snapshot automation is so named because it is not a dynamic process, but instead captures existing settings at a particular instant in time. This is very helpful if you want a sudden change, rather than a change that fades in or out over time. For example with mix levels, you could set your faders to the desired levels at the beginning of the big chorus and then take a snapshot of that setting. Those levels will remain in effect until you either take another snapshot or start recording automation by some other method.

Method 5: Using Level-Riding Plug-Ins

One of the main goals of mixing vocals is to make sure they're always intelligible. However if set for a static level, a vocal might be too loud during quiet parts, yet be masked by other instruments during loud passages.

For years, the way to overcome this was for an engineer to ride the fader while mixing, adjusting the vocal level manually, in real time. By doing so, the engineer could make sure the vocal was always at the appropriate level. Level-riding plug-ins such as Waves Vocal Rider do this automatically so that the vocal remains at a target level you specify (see Fig. 7.4)—just as if you were riding the fader manually.

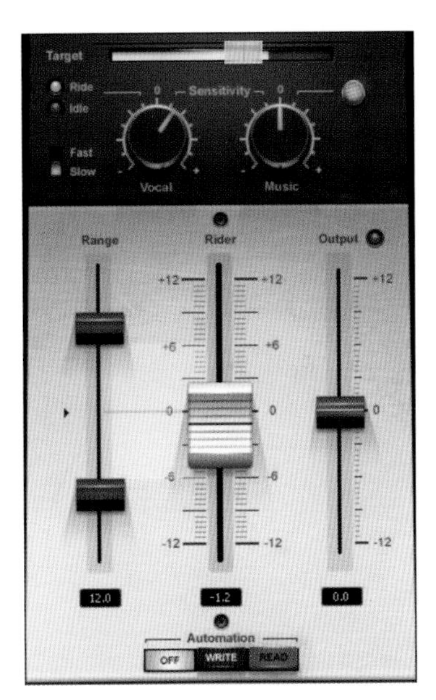

Figure 7.4 Vocal Rider maintains a consistent vocal level and can react to the overall mix via side-chaining.

Vocal Rider also writes corresponding automation, so you can edit the automation (for example, to bring up a vocal more in the chorus) if the background music changes levels. It can use the vocal itself as a reference to maintain a consistent output, or make adjustments based on a reference signal appearing at a sidechain input. If this reference represents the entire mix (minus the vocal being processed), then the vocal level will change based on the level of the mix itself—getting louder in louder passages and softer in softer passages.

The main advantage of using vocal riding programs to even out levels compared to compression is that vocal riders don't alter the fidelity or moment-to-moment dynamics, just the overall level—there's no more processing than you'd have by moving a fader.

So are they a panacea? Yes and no. For narration or audio books, where a consistent voice level is crucial, vocal gain-riding plug-ins are worth their weight in gold. For music, it depends on the music itself. These programs can't make artistic decisions, only technical ones, so you will always have more control by riding gain manually and making edits to your automation. However, they can save a lot of time by providing an intelligent first pass at automation, which you can then edit further for those sections where you might disagree with the software's decisions.

Automating Effects

The same techniques that you use to automate levels, panning, and the like also apply to effects. This can be particularly useful with vocals—for example, to bring delay effects in and out or to alter reverb decays.

Key Takeaways

- It's important that the vocals be intelligible but not overpowering. Automation helps achieve this goal by raising and lowering the vocal level automatically as needed throughout the song.
- Automation can also work with effects like EQ, reverb, dynamics, echo, and the like. This can help make vocals more varied and interesting.
- Some plug-ins adjust vocal levels automatically either to hit a consistent level or to react based on what else is happening with the music.

Chapter 8

Double-Tracking, Harmonizing, and Layering Vocals

Double-tracking a vocal is the process of singing an additional, duplicate vocal on top of a main vocal to thicken the overall sound. Doubled vocals are typically mixed around –3 to –10 dB behind the main vocal to avoid competing with it. Because it's impossible to sing a vocal exactly the same way twice, there will be slight timing and pitch differences that add interest and depth. The potential tradeoff is that a doubled vocal may sound a little less focused, but sometimes that's exactly the effect you want.

Automatic Double-Tracking (ADT) Plug-Ins

Although it's easy enough to re-record a vocal, some vocalists have a hard time reproducing exactly what they sang. For these situations, there are plug-ins that can process the original track by introducing the pitch and timing variations associated with double tracking (Fig. 8.1).

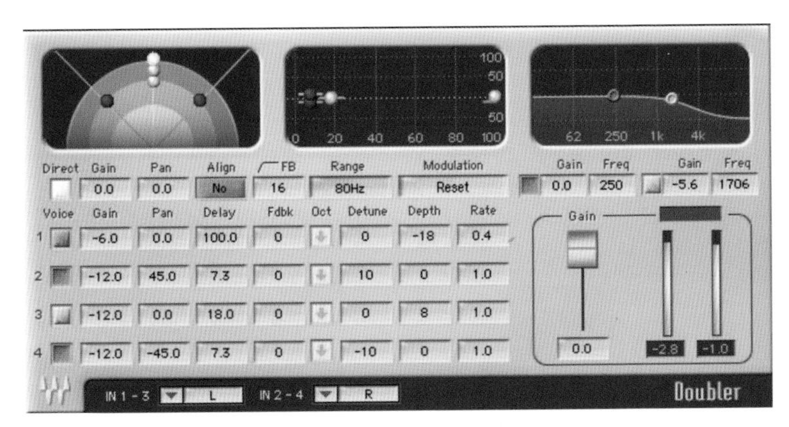

Figure 8.1 The Doubler plug-in from Waves can generate up to four double-tracked lines, each with their own variations, based on a single vocal.

Pseudo-ADT with Pitch Correction

Although dedicated plug-ins like the one above can provide double tracking, many people are surprised to find that pitch correction software has the necessary tools to provide electronically generated doubling effects. The following example is based on Celemony Melodyne, but the principle is the same for other pitch-correction software.

When using pitch correction software, the doubling effect works best with vocals that don't already have extensive pitch or timing correction.

To set up the doubling effect with Melodyne:

1. Duplicate the original, uncorrected vocal track.
2. Open the track in Melodyne. Note that programs with ARA (Audio Random Access, a protocol created by Celemony and PreSonus) can typically open Melodyne like any other clip effect.
3. Select all the notes in the vocal.
4. Turn up Correct Pitch Center to about 60%.
5. Turn up Quantize Time Intensity to about 60%.
6. Audition the ADT effect.
7. If necessary, tweak the pitch and timing correction amounts for the most realistic results.

You generally don't want the doubled vocal to have too much pitch or timing correction—just enough to be different from the main vocal (see Fig. 8.2).

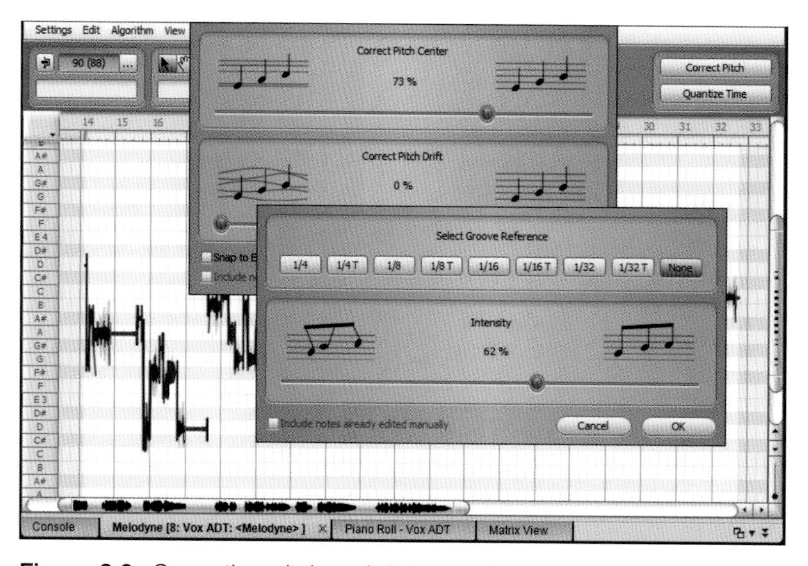

Figure 8.2 Correcting pitch and timing subtly on a duplicated vocal track can produce an automatic double-tracking effect.

Shifting Pitch to Create Pseudo-Double Tracking

This trick is as old as the Eventide Harmonizer (trademark Eventide), when engineers discovered that shifting pitch downward and mixing the harmonized signal behind the unprocessed vocal added a useful thickening effect. You can do this with any hardware or software pitch-shifting processor. If you want to triple the vocal, add a second pitch shifter and shift up by an amount equal to the downward shift of the first pitch shifter. When tripling, you may want to increase the overall amount of shift in each direction.

Here's how to create this effect.

1. Copy the vocal track you want to thicken, so you now have two tracks of the same vocal.
2. Apply a pitch shift plug-in or hardware processor to one of the tracks. A good starting point for pitch shifting is –15 to –30 cents.

   Altenatively, you may be able to detune the track itself, if the option exists (Fig. 8.3). In this case, you won't need to use a separate plug-in.

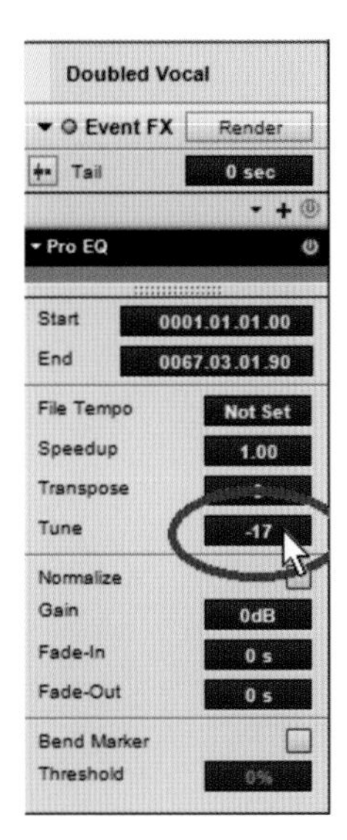

Figure 8.3 Studio One Pro's Inspector allows easy detuning for pitch-shifting effects.

3. If using a plug-in, set the mix parameter to 100% processed sound (you want only the pitch-shifted sound). If the plug-in has a feedback parameter, set it to 0.
4. If delay time and modulation are available, try modulating pitch very slowly over a range of about 3 to 15 ms. This adds a bit of variety.
5. Mix the doubled track down so it doesn't compete with, but instead complements, the lead vocal.

How to Mix Double-Tracked Vocals

When mixing, centering the two vocals gives an effect similar to chorusing; the vocals sound somewhat more diffused, which works well for gentler material. This also gives the thickest sound. Panning them slightly opposed (about 30% right and 30% left) can give a more spacious sound in stereo, and sounds more like two individual vocals instead of a composite effect (which may or not be what you want).

With sparser mixes, centered panning often works best; for dense material, like hard rock with lots of distorted guitar, spreading the sound somewhat gives the vocals more presence. However, these aren't rules, because ultimately, the song itself will dictate what works best in the final mix. Besides, you can automate the panning to place the vocals as appropriate for particular parts of the song.

The Doubled Vocal Fix

Suppose you've recorded a really great doubled vocal part, but unfortunately, for one short phrase only one of the two tracks has a perfect take. One way to fix this is to copy the perfect part into the other track, then delay it by 20 to 35 ms. This will be just enough to make it sound like it's a doubled vocal (see Fig. 8.4).

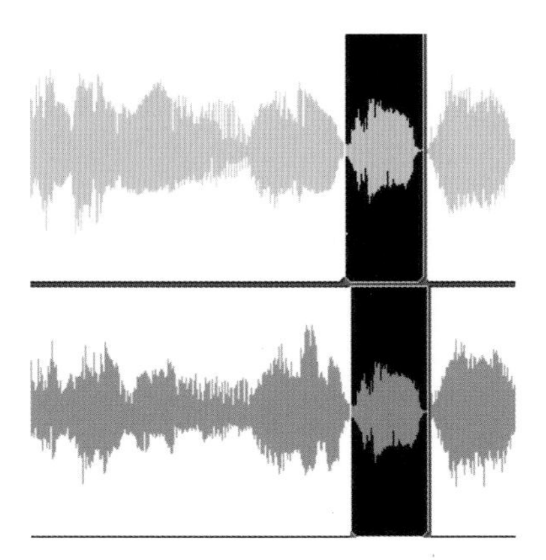

Figure 8.4 Copying part of a vocal from one track and offsetting it slightly can replace a sketchy note in a different track.

Creating Harmonies with Pitch Correction Software

When you can't quite hit the high or low notes, or your voice loses power at extreme pitch ranges, pitch correction software can usually help by applying pitch transposition. (There are limitations, though; transposing too far can give an unnatural effect).

If you don't have a wide vocal range, you may have to choose a vocal's key very carefully to make sure you can hit the high harmony notes; however, this might compromise the sound of the low notes, pushing them out of your comfort zone. This is where pitch correction can help. You can use pitch correction to fix high notes that are just a bit out of your range, allowing you to choose the optimum key for the lead vocal and use pitch correction where needed for the harmony.

Most of the time, I can hit the harmonies, so I'll sing them and bring in pitch correction to the harmony if needed. But there's also merit to using pitch correction to generate a harmony electronically, even when you can hit the notes—the timbre has a different character that works well in some musical contexts. Another benefit is that you can experiment with synthesizing different harmony parts, then learn to sing them and replace the synthesized versions.

Here's how to create harmonies using Celemony's Melodyne essential, although the same basic principles apply to other pitch-correction software:

1. Duplicate the lead vocal.
2. Open the lead vocal in Melodyne (programs that include the Audio Random Access protocol can typically open Melodyne like any other clip effect).
3. Solo the lead vocal and the duplicated vocal. Your host software's dim solo function can be useful for this application so you can hear the vocals along with the rest of the song.

Dim solo functionality is described in Chapter 2 of this book.

4. Adjust the pitch of the duplicate track's blobs to create the harmony (see Fig. 8.5).

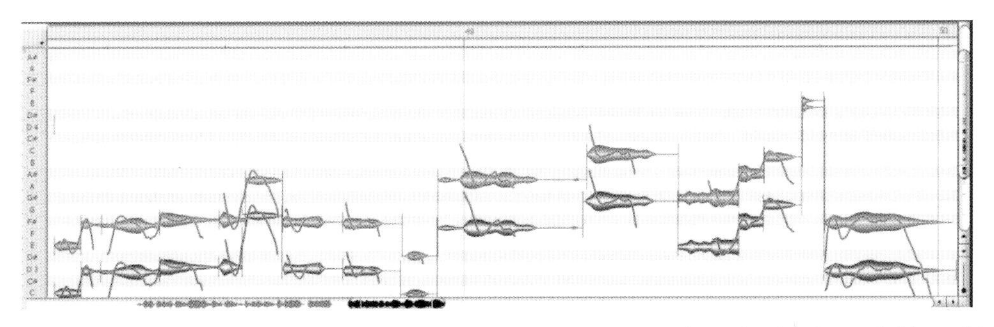

Figure 8.5 The harmony line in Melodyne (blue) superimposed on the lead vocal. Note: Melodyne does not display tracks superimposed like this; the screenshot has been altered to help visualize the effect.

Often the easiest way to create a harmony like this is by ear; however even the basic version of Melodyne (Melodyne essential) can display different reference scales indicating where the scale steps fall. If you're theory minded, you can always apply the rules of harmony to determine which pitches to use for your harmonies. Also consider turning off chromatic snapping for pitch, and adjust the harmony pitch by ear. Sometimes you might want the harmony just a little bit sharp or flat to add a little more tension.

Feel free to combine this process with the previous suggestions for creating pseudo-automatic double tracking with pitch correction. Applying those techniques to the harmony line can help establish it as an independent entity.

Techniques for Layered Vocals

Layering vocals—singing multiple vocals and stacking them on top of each other—is a common technique to thicken a vocal part, whether applied to a solo voice or to a massed group of backing vocals. However, there are certain considerations with layered vocals that don't apply to single vocals, because layered vocals need to have a coherent, solid vibe. Words can't start or end at different times, unless you're going for a certain looseness. For tight vocals, there are several DAW techniques that can give the kind of feel you want.

Dealing with Inhales

Inhales are a natural part of singing; however with multiple voices, inhales often don't occur simultaneously. For a more unified sound, pick two inhales that are in sync (or just one, if there aren't two together), and delete the other ones by cutting from the start of the inhale to where the note begins. Adding a slight fade at the edits will make for a smoother transition, although the inhales you've kept will likely smooth over these transitions anyway.

If you want to keep an inhale but find that it's too prominent, try fading in on the inhale to make it less obtrusive while still retaining an authentic vocal quality.

Fixing Notes That Don't End at the Same Time

If one note is short compared to another that's the correct length, split the short clip just before the last word, and use the host program's DSP time-stretching function to lengthen that one word. In some cases you can split a note during the note's sustain, stretch the end longer, and then crossfade the split region to make a smooth transition between the main part and the note's sustaining end. This can give a more natural sound if you need a fair amount of correction.

A note that extends too long is easier to fix—just fade it so its length matches the reference vocal, or split during a sustain and move the end closer to the beginning, with crossfade enabled to provide a smooth transition between the two. For a really uniform sound, group all the vocal clips together and add a common fade so that they all fade simultaneously. This creates a super-precise vocal sound, but because you're not processing the vocal itself, the sound is natural (see Fig. 8.6).

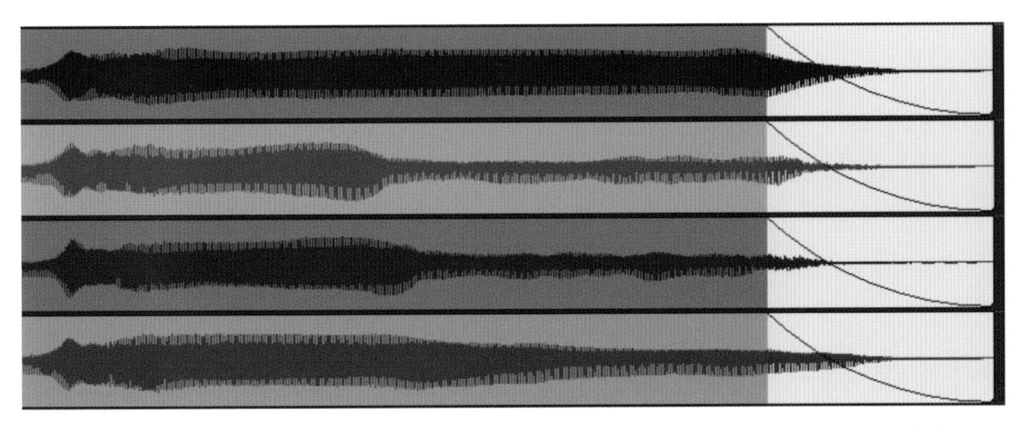

Figure 8.6 Each word has been aligned to start at the same time, while a common fade time creates a common ending. Before the fades were added, the notes had different end times.

Shifting Vocal Formants

Formants determine vocal timbre, and different people's voices exhibit different timbres because of their vocal formants. For example, Mickey Mouse's formant produces a bright, high timbre, while Darth Vader's formant creates a timbre that's dark and low.

You can add variety to vocals by changing the vocal formats, particularly if you're singing all the layered vocal background parts yourself. For example, if you're singing three background vocal parts, you might want to give one of them a brighter formant and another a darker formant. Formant editing isn't that common with software, although Melodyne's editor and studio versions provide formant editing options.

Back in the days of tape, a common technique to change vocal formants was slowing down the tape somewhat, singing to the slowed-down track, then speeding it back up again. This brightened up the voice's formant, and had the side benefit of tightening up the timing. Most recording software has some way to vary pitch, either for the project as a whole or for individual clips. If you can change the project tempo, then you can use the same technique as tape: slow down the project (or speed it up, if you want the vocal to sound deeper), sing along, then bring the project speed back to pitch.

Bussing

To avoid having to mix multiple vocal tracks simultaneously, set up aux sends in each of the layered vocals, and have each send terminate in a single stereo return. Not only does this make it a lot easier to mix because you need adjust only the single return instead of all the individual tracks, but you can also use a common signal processor (like a bus compressor set for a modest amount of compression) to "glue" the layered tracks together. A bussed, individual stereo output also lends itself well to reverb, because the voices sound like they're in a common acoustical space.

If you don't need a common effect on all the tracks, an alternate to bussing is to *group* the track levels together so that varying one fader varies all faders in the group.

Key Takeaways

- Doubling vocals is a popular technique, but be careful about setting levels—the doubled track should support the main vocal, not compete with it, unless you want a more diffused vocal effect.
- Pitch correction software can also produce automatic double-tracking effects.
- If you can't quite hit the harmony notes, you can choose to correct existing notes with pitch correction or even transpose a copy of your main vocal to synthesize a harmony.
- When layering vocals, having common start times and fadeouts produces a tighter sound.

Chapter 9

Vocal Performance Tips

Most technology books pretty much stick to technology, which is fine... but music is about emotion, and that starts with you—not a mic, preamp, or hard disk recording program. The most important aspect of recording vocals isn't your gear, it's your mental and physical state when you hit the record button. I hope some of these tips will help improve your performance so that you can be happy, not just with the sound of your recordings, but with their emotional impact as well.

Emotional Dynamic Range

I feel the concept of dynamic range can apply to emotional variations, not just level variations. Vocals are the emotional focus of most popular music, yet many self-produced songs don't pay enough attention to the voice's crucial importance. Part of this is due to the difficulty of being objective enough to produce your own vocals. I've been fortunate to work with some great producers over the years, and I've learned some important points to remember when producing my own projects. So, let's look at a way to step back and put more emotional dynamic range into your vocals.

The Lyric Sheet

Some think it's cheating to write out the lyrics, but there may be more to the story than that. Michael Stewart (who produced Billy Joel's "Piano Man") found he often obtained better performances from players when their conscious minds were focused on something other than playing, like looking at a picture or text. It kept them from being judgmental about the performance—they just played. A lyric sheet can help with this. Another trick from Michael, for singers who play an instrument, is to have the singer play along while singing (without recording the instrument).

I use a lyric sheet in the studio not because I can't remember the words, but because it allows me to not even have to try to remember them. That means one less potential source of distraction. A lyric sheet also provides a kind of roadmap because no matter how well you know the words to a song, the lyric sheet can guide your delivery through the piece.

You may not even have to look at what you wrote—the process of writing out the lyrics may be all you need. However, consider taking this process further: Grab two different colored pens and analyze the lyrics. Underline words or phrases that should be emphasized in one color (e.g., blue), and words that are crucial to the point of the song in the other color (e.g., red). For example, here are notes on the second verse for a song of mine from several years ago (see Fig. 9.1).

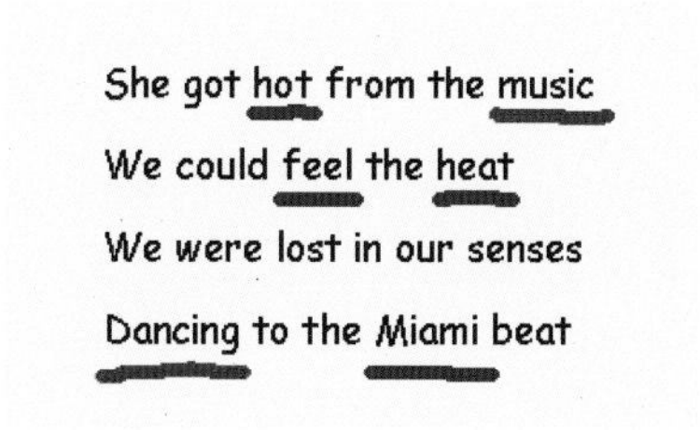

She got hot from the music

We could feel the heat

We were lost in our senses

Dancing to the Miami beat

Figure 9.1 Analyze your lyrics as a producer would to make sure you maximize the effectiveness of every word.

In the first line, "hot" is an attention-getting word and rhymes with "got," so it receives emphasis. As the song concerns a relationship that revs up because of dancing and music, "music" is crucial to the point of the song and receives added emphasis.

In line 2, "feel" and "heat" get emphasis, especially because "heat" refers back to "hot," and is foreshadowing to "beat" in the fourth line.

Line 3 doesn't get a huge emphasis, because it provides the breather before hitting the payoff line, which includes the title of the song ("The Miami Beat"). "Dancing" has major emphasis; "Miami beat" gets less because it re-appears several times in the tune... no point in wearing out its welcome.

By going through a song line by line, you'll have a better idea of where/how to make the song tell a story, create a flow from beginning to end, and emphasize the most important elements. Also, going over the lyrics with a fine-tooth comb is good quality control to make sure every word counts.

Ways to Add Emphasis

Emphasis is not just about singing louder. Here are other ways to emphasize a word or phrase.

Bend Pitch

Words with bent pitch will stand out compared to notes sung straight. Singers will often start above or below the target pitch; then slide to it quickly to add more emphasis.

Clipped vs. Sustained

Following a clipped series of notes with sustained sounds tends to raise the emotional level. Think of Sam and Dave's song "Soul Man": The verses are pretty clipped, but when they go into "I'm a soul man," they really draw out "soul man." The contrast with the more percussive singing in the verses is dramatic.

Throat vs. Lungs

Pushing air from the throat sounds very different compared to drawing air from the lungs. The breathier throat sound is good for setting up a fuller, louder, lung-driven sound. ABBA's "Dancing Queen" highlights some of these techniques: the section of the song starting with "Friday night and the lights are low" is breathier and more clipped (although the ends of lines tend to be more sustained). As the song moves toward the "Dancing Queen" and "You can dance" climax, the notes sustain longer and are less breathy.

Timbre Changes

Changing your voice's timbre draws attention to it. (David Bowie was a master of this technique.) Doubling a vocal line can make a voice seem stronger, but try placing the doubled vocal back in the mix compared to the main vocal—enough to support, not compete.

Vibrato

Vibrato is often overused to add emphasis. You don't need to add much; think of jazz trumpeter Miles Davis. He almost never used vibrato, electing instead to use well-placed pitch-bending. (Granted, he wasn't a singer—but he used his trumpet in a very vocal manner.) Vibrato often fades out just before the note ends, like pulling back the mod wheel on a synthesizer. This adds a sense of closure that completes a phrase.

"Better" Is Not Always Better

Paradoxically, really good vocalists sometimes find it difficult to hit a wide emotional dynamic range because they have the chops to sing at full blast, all the time. This is particularly true with singers who come from a stage background and are used to singing for the back row. Lesser vocalists often make up for a lack of technical skill by craftier performances, and fully exploiting the tools they have. If you have a great voice, that's terrific—but don't end up like the guitarist who can play a zillion notes a second but ultimately has nothing to say. Pull back and let your performance breathe.

Every Word Matters

Vocals are the primary human-to-human connection in a great deal of popular music, so reflect on every word because *every* word is important. If some words simply don't work, it's better to revise the song rather than rely on vocal technique or artifice to carry you through.

Avoiding the Vocal Disconnect

The purpose of a vocal is to connect with your audience. But clearly, not all singers succeed. A lack of connection with an audience often reflects a lack of connection within the singer—if the singer doesn't bond with the vocal, there's no way the audience is going to bond with the singer. This can be a major problem in the studio, where you have no audience to prompt you to remain connected to the vocal.

Following are some ways to prompt yourself to remain connected to the lyrics. Hopefully in the process, you'll connect better with your listeners.

Fusion: It's the Package

As obvious as it may sound, remember that music and lyrics are a single package: One of a vocalist's main tasks is to integrate the two into a single experience. To put it in technical terms, music and lyrics are each separate data streams, and the singer multiplexes them into a single, cohesive statement. Or you can think of the melody as the carrier, and the words as the modulator. In any event, the point is that you must never emphasize one element at the expense of the other.

Aretha Franklin is an outstanding example of someone who fuses lyrics and melody into a single entity. Bob Dylan is another one, whose quirky lyrics match his quirky voice; or consider Bob Marley, whose vocals were sometimes closer to a percussive instrument.

To hear examples of people who *don't* fuse music and lyrics, just tune in to any American Idol-type show when they're auditioning singers. Some of the performers are so into screaming and over-emoting with their voice they forget that they're also supposed to be telling a story. Sometimes I almost feel you could go up to these people and ask, "What were you singing about?" and they wouldn't be able to answer.

Theatrical actors know they have to make grander gestures than in real life; I feel singing works the same way. When people hear your voice, they can't see your face or feel your vibe. Throw a little extra into your performance (as long as it's genuine!) to make up for the "emotion loss" that occurs from recording.

Surprise—You're a Salesperson

When you're singing, you're a salesperson. You need to *sell* the listener that you believe in what you're singing, that you know how to sing, and that you're worth listening to.

They say the best salespeople are those who believe in the product they're selling, and that includes singing. But this doesn't just mean confidence; plenty of lousy singers truly believe they're great. Of course, believing in yourself never hurts, but believing in the *song* is key. There's no point in singing lyrics you don't believe in, whether it's a cover song or something you wrote. If you ever find yourself simply going through the motions when singing a song, don't bother taking the time to record it.

Intimacy

When singing live, eye contact is crucial for establishing a connection with the audience. For me, the most amazing aspect of being on stage is all those eyes looking back at me—which immediately makes me want to look into the eyes of everyone there. We're human; we long for contact and communication. Singing to people means you not only have to believe in the song, you have to believe that someone else will, too.

It may sound impossible to simulate that experience in the studio... and it is. However, there are technical ways to increase intimacy, as we've already covered: Use the proximity effect to add bass and warmth, make the vocal more present with phrase-by-phrase normalization or gain processing, and/or use compression or limiting to bring your sound closer to the listener.

Generally, intimacy implies a natural, close-up sound—something almost conversational in nature (although possibly a loud conversation!). But intimacy has other facets. Sometimes the way the voice connects is by being distant and ethereal—sounding more like a voice from inside the listener, rather than being outside the listener (for a prominent example of this style, think Enya). It's even possible to combine both; this is something Dido does well, with a voice that's both evocative and yet conversational.

Wait Until Playback Before You Judge Yourself

When you cut a vocal, turn off the internal critic that apparently lives in just about every artist's head. Don't attempt to judge yourself when you sing. Don't think, "On my next take, I need to sing that phrase better."

It's harder to turn this off than you might think, because self-judgment happens almost subconsciously—you'll probably find that once you become conscious of that internal critic, first you'll curse me for making you aware of something you now can't ignore, and second, you'll discover that it's hard to turn off.

But you really do need to turn it off. Remember, you're selling that vocal to the listener, not just yourself. Put everything you have into projecting that vocal outward. Listen to yourself only enough to make sure you're on target; put all your energies into your voice. It's like baseball: You don't look at the bat, you look at the ball and you naturally move the bat to hit it. Always keep the end listener in mind, and your vocal will flow naturally toward that goal.

The Performance Curve

There will be some nights when you record yourself, or someone else, and everything sounds great. And there will be other nights when nothing sounds great. Why is this? What's the difference?

The essence of recording vocals comes down capturing great performances. All related tools, techniques, and technologies become irrelevant without that crucial element. Although the right tools can help promote a better performance—like loop-based recording to get a vocalist into a groove—ultimately a good performance also has to do with production skills and knowing how to get the most out of a performer. The question is whether you can find some quantifiable element that will help in getting the best possible take.

Although this book is intended more for those who record themselves, you may record others as well, and you may find that identifying a vocalist's type can be very helpful. And if you can identify one of these types for *yourself* as a vocalist, it may help you realize when you'll be at your peak. Knowing your type will also help you understand when to warm up, when to take a break, and when to call it a night.

I've worked with a lot of artists over the years. I've found that certain artists tended to reach peaks at a particular time in the process of recording their takes. The following charts describe the different types of performance patterns I've encountered in the studio.

The Double Peak

Observing what happens with my own performances when recording vocal parts and picking the best sections, I found that the quality of takes follows a definite pattern. The first couple takes are pretty good. Then they start to go downhill before taking an upward path again. Eventually they hit a peak that sometimes exceeds the initial one. Then past a certain point, they deteriorate at a pretty rapid rate. I call this a *double-peak* curve because it has a peak at the beginning, and a peak toward the end (see Fig. 9.2). It's uncanny how often this happens... and this isn't limited to vocals, it also happens when I'm playing an instrument.

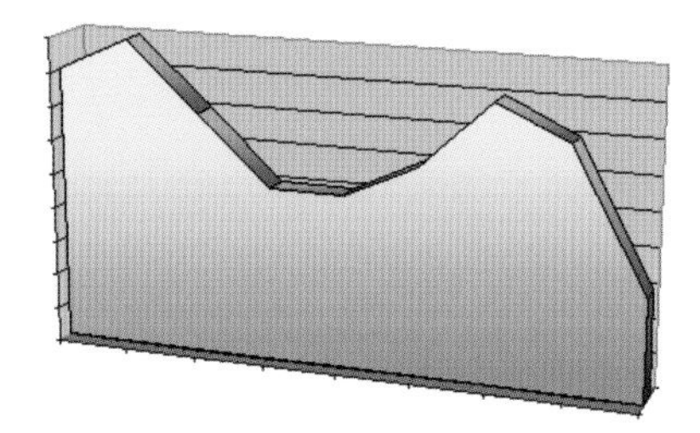

Figure 9.2 With the double-peak performance curve, you usually want to catch the second peak.

The Quick Starter

This performer starts strong, has several good takes in a row, then doesn't really improve on the performance over time. Many times, these are musicians who play live a lot. They're conditioned to get things right and give it their all out of the gate because live, you get only one chance (see Fig. 9.3).

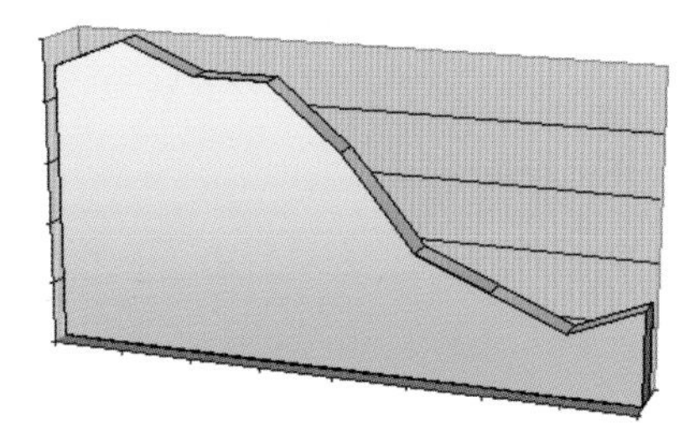

Figure 9.3 Make sure you're in record mode as soon as a quick starter steps up to the mic to capture the first several takes.

The Long Ramp-Up

Some performers take a while to warm up and get into the groove. This often happens with musicians who compose in the studio. As they feel their way around the part, they become more comfortable with it. After they hit their stride, sometimes you'll get a killer take; sometimes you'll get a series of takes that are all pretty good and when composited together, produce a definitive performance (see Fig. 9.4).

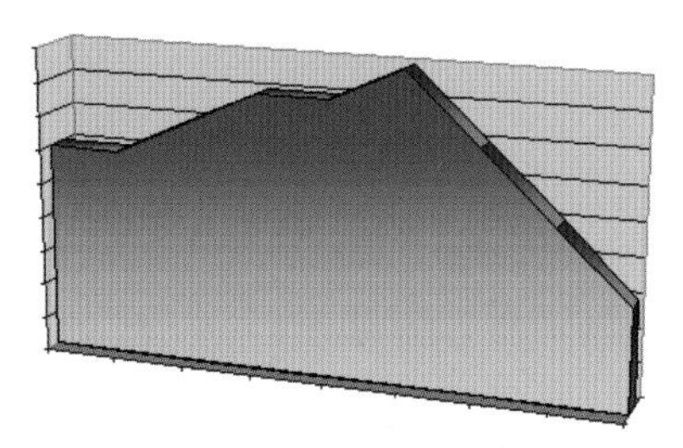

Figure 9.4 With this kind of performer, avoid putting on any pressure or being too critical early on. Give them some space.

The Anything Goes

This is the kind of performer who goes strictly from the gut. Rather than follow a particular curve over the course of several takes, they hit high and low points within individual takes, as the mood hits them. These are the most time-consuming performances for composite recording, because you might end up taking different phrases from early, middle, and late takes. Yet the final results can be really good, because there are a series of spontaneous moments that produce multiple high points during a take.

In any event, make sure the final performance breathes and has some less-intense sections to provide contrast with the moments of high emotion. With these people, record *everything* because you never know when the great take is going to happen (see Fig. 9.5).

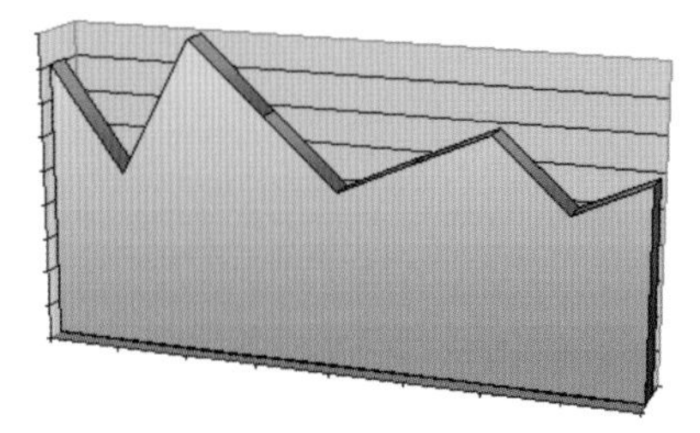

Figure 9.5 Make sure you have plenty of free disk space when you start recording an anything goes performer.

The Rock Steady

I first encountered this type with the late classical guitarist Linda Cohen. All her takes were consistently good, so the only real question was whether she could do one that was better. What I like best about this kind of performer is you can do takes of lots of different songs during a session, because you don't have to spend too much time on any one song (see Fig. 9.6).

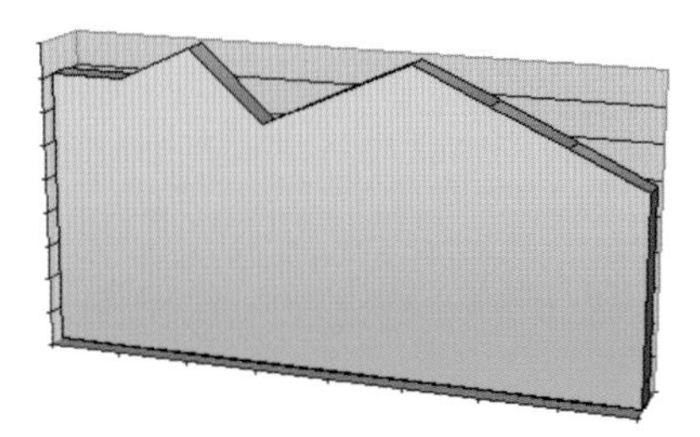

Figure 9.6 Performers who follow this kind of curve are rare... be grateful when you get a chance to record one.

There are other patterns as well, but these are main ones I've recognized over the years. While identifying types may sound a bit abstract, there are practical ramifications. For example, Linda knew when she had done a good take, at which point she would tend to want to move on (classical guitarists don't get huge budgets for studio time, so time is of the essence). I usually agreed with her. But on one occasion I had heard her do a tune better in rehearsal than she had done it in the studio, even though her take was technically flawless. I wanted to ask her to do another take, but knew she'd think it was superfluous.

So speaking into the talkback mic, I said that unfortunately the record button hadn't been enabled on her previous take. She was kind of bummed, but being a pro, she did another take. However, my "mistake" sort of shook things up; while her part was again perfect, it had a little more feel. Of course, the previous take *had* actually been recorded, so if the newer one hadn't been as good, there wouldn't have been any problem.

However—you wouldn't try that approach with a long ramp-up-type performer, because it takes them so long to get where they're going that they'd likely strangle you if they thought you'd made such a major mistake. With their type of curve, you're best off saying, "The last take was really good, but they keep getting better, so let's try just one more."

The quick starter type is something else. If the takes aren't happening, I prefer to move on to a different song entirely, and return to the one where I want a better take at a later time. Coming back to it seems to reboot this type and takes advantage of their quick starter mentality.

For the anything goes-type vocalist, I usually don't ask for new takes, but tend to go more for punches in specific sections. ("That was good, but I think we need a bit more energy when the second verse comes in.") These performers seem to break performances down into smaller pieces rather than thinking in terms of takes, so they fit well with a punch-in oriented approach.

With the double peak type, as long as the takes keep getting better in the second series of peaks, I keep recording. Once two or three takes in a row don't improve on previous takes, it's time to move on. It's unlikely that this type is going to get anything more that's worth recording.

The Volume Jump Trick

Here's a sneaky trick I was taught by an extremely talented engineer: Just when you think you're about to peak, turn up the headphone volume ever so slightly—no more than a dB or so. This raises your energy level an extra little bit, and often inspires what ends up being the best take.

But you only get one or possibly two chances to do this. It's the novelty of the change that makes the difference. So, you have to gauge precisely when your Cartier-Bresson-like perfect moment is about to occur. Knowing the performance curve helps you decide. With an anything goes performer, I wait until I have enough takes in the can that I know it's possible to put together a good part. Then I'll goose the volume a tad and do a few more takes. Sometimes these are ideal for adding that slight extra edge on the final verse or chorus or wherever.

The long ramp-up type is the most difficult to anticipate. You have to choose the moment that's just before their best take. Some performers have such consistent performance curves you can almost do it by the numbers—for example, you know that the ninth or tenth take is almost always the best one. In other cases, you just have to trust your feelings about when to do the boost.

With a double peak performer, it's usually pretty obvious when the second peak is happening. That's when to do the level boost.

For the quick starter, I record a take or two, then bump up the volume a tad to see if I can get that magic take just before things start to fade. For the rock steady, I'll say, "Okay, we have what we need, but let's do one more for luck," and turn up the volume a bit. Hey, if it gets a good performance, that's what counts.

Break Time

The performance curve also influences when each performer should take a short break, which most musicians feel the need to do occasionally during the course of a session. With the quick starter type, it helps to have a glass of water already set up next to the mic; once you start, you don't want to stop. The long ramp-up performer can sometimes benefit from working breaks into the process. This seems to impart a somewhat fresh perspective when the performer returns; they'll proceed in the direction they were going, but with a slightly different vibe. This may give more options in the final composite performance (e.g., you can drop in the second verse from one of the post-break takes to add a bit more variety).

With the double-peak type, the best place to take a break is if the second peak is slow in coming. Sometimes a break will "break the ice" and cause the second peak to shake loose. If it doesn't, then it's probably best to move on to a different tune. Sometimes the planets just are not in alignment to do the perfect performance—part of producing is recognizing when that happens.

That's a Take

Yes, there are a lot of variables—the above are simply guidelines to get you thinking rather than ironclad rules. Having said that, once you become aware of this phenomenon, you might be surprised at how often it *is* an ironclad rule. Just like some people are night people and some are day people, it seems some people settle naturally into a performance curve that doesn't vary much, if at all.

So next time you're recording, see if one of these performance curves fits the vocalist. You may be able to use that knowledge to your advantage.

About the Author

Musician/author Craig Anderton is an internationally recognized authority on music and technology. His onstage career spans from the 60s with the group Mandrake, through the early 2000s with electronic groups Air Liquide and Rei$$dorf Force, to the "power duo" EV2 with Public Enemy's Brian Hardgroove, and EDM-oriented solo performances.

He has played on, produced, or mastered over 20 major label recordings, did pop music session work in New York in the 1970s on guitar and keyboards, played Carnegie Hall, and more recently, has mastered well over a hundred tracks for various artists.

In the mid-80s, Craig co-founded *Electronic Musician* magazine. As an author, he's written over 26 books on musical electronics and over a thousand articles for magazines like *Keyboard, Sound on Sound, Rolling Stone, Pro Sound News, Guitar Player, Mix,* and several European publications.

Craig has lectured on technology and the arts (in 10 countries, 38 U.S. states, and three languages), and done sound design work for companies like Alesis, Gibson, Peavey, PreSonus, Roland, and Steinberg.

Please check out some of his music at youtube.com/thecraiganderton, visit his web site at craiganderton.com, and follow him on twitter @craig_anderton.